COURAGE

The Story of
Sir James Dunn

BOOKS BY
LORD BEAVERBROOK

Canada in Flanders (2 volumes)
Success
Politicians and the Press
Politicians and the War (2 volumes)
Resources of the British Empire
Don't Trust to Luck
Three Keys to Success
Men and Power
Friends
Courage

LORD BEAVERBROOK

COURAGE

The Story of
Sir James Dunn

BRUNSWICK PRESS
FREDERICTON NEW BRUNSWICK CANADA

ACKNOWLEDGMENTS

LADY DUNN PUT at my disposal all the papers, records and documents of her husband, Sir James Dunn. She has not held back or withdrawn any pieces of paper in the immense collection, possibly far exceeding any other private archives in all Canada, excluding, of course, the public Minutes of our Prime Ministers and others engaged in Government.

She has permitted the use of her own diaries for my guidance in the interpretation of material.

I wish to thank her too for permission to publish several of her letters. And she has allowed me to reproduce my choice of her husband's letters to her.

I must thank the Estates of Sir William Van Horne and Sir William Orpen.

Mr. T. R. McLagan, Mr. S. W. Alexander and Mr. George MacLeod have given me permission to quote from their writings.

The curator of the Frick Collection has given me valuable and useful information about paintings, formerly the property of Sir James Dunn and sold by him in the years of distress.

Several friends have assisted me in researching and recording the vast collection of documents. Mr. George Malcolm Thomson has, as usual, read my proofs, at the same time made many corrections.

Miss Jean Riley and Miss Rosemary Brooks have been constant and devoted helpers. They have kept my records in order, and have been remembrancers. They have compiled and made précis of documents and files. These have been of immense value.

To my friends and fellow workers I owe my grateful thanks.

BEAVERBROOK

Blessed shalt thou be when thou comest in, and blessed shalt thou be when thou goest out.

—Deuteronomy

INSCRIPTION

This is the story of Sir James Dunn, Ironmaster, a native of New Brunswick.

At the age of 61, he entered on his kingdom of steel and he ruled it until he died at 81.

In the space of over 20 years he built up a self-contained and personally controlled steel industry.

By the development of ore bodies he fired all Canada with enthusiasm for exploration and research, sparking many projects that have increased and multiplied the mineral wealth of the country.

His life story is a resounding example of what can be accomplished by men of mature years, for he showed that old age need impose no barrier to achievement, no limit to vision.

On the evening of his death he was about to launch a 20 years' programme, which would have exalted his steelworks to a position of world-wide importance.

Twice he was on the brink of ruin. He saved himself by his own efforts and his own strength of character.

Twice he was in danger of death, when he sustained a coronary thrombosis, followed by a major operation in his 70th year.

This brief narrative is a tribute to a man's courage and a record of triumph in old age that will bring comfort and confidence to many a reader.

CONTENTS

page

ILLUSTRATIONS

INTRODUCTION

From quiet homes and first beginning,
Out to the undiscovered ends,
There's nothing worth the wear of winning
But laughter and the love of friends.

—BELLOC

THE REMOTE AND inhospitable Province of New Brunswick, as I knew it at the close of the 19th Century, did not appear to be a promising breeding ground for eminent men destined for great achievements of different kinds.

Yet, in one generation, New Brunswick produced three such men, all of whom were close friends of mine.

They were Andrew Bonar Law, Richard Bedford Bennett and James Hamet Dunn.

It is of James Dunn that I write this memoir with the intention of attempting to describe the character and conduct of this great leader of men, foremost industrialist in Canada.

He was generous to an amazing extent, but sometimes difficult, unjust and even harsh in the interpretation of his responsibilities.

He was loyal to his friends and employees. Yet he was sometimes brash in his treatment of faithful supporters.

He sustained and endured bitter hostilities

and repelled serious attacks which might have ruined him in the midst of his triumphs. But he had no hesitation in reconciling himself to his enemies and indeed showering benefits upon them.

He had wealth abounding in his old age. Yet he was short of funds in mid journey through life and often seriously embarrassed. Once in the First World War and again in the second War he was in danger of disaster if creditors had insisted upon payment of debts beyond his immediate resources.

He surpassed in gorgeous living many a Doge of Venice. Yet he would be satisfied with simple and healthy recreations.

The splendour of his dinners with champagne and caviar at the Pavillon in New York was in contrast to his soup and rice ration at his home in Dayspring with a mixed drink of milk and water. His physical endurance was remarkable and he was convinced that long life was his portion. Yet he should have known that his days were numbered when he sustained three serious surgical operations and a coronary thrombosis in his last 15 years.

All in all he was a most interesting companion and a most competent man of business.

He was endowed with industry and judgment and a sure and certain capacity for avoiding self deception. He also had courage, exceeding that of any man I have known.

Though James Dunn was my boyhood friend

and staunch companion through life, I did not hold him first among equals.

It was to Andrew Bonar Law that I gave my absolute devotion. He was more than a friend, much more. He was a man to whom I gave my total personal and political allegiance without qualification or reserve. He was my leader. I was his follower.

Bonar Law was the only man from the Dominions to become Prime Minister of Great Britain. His untimely death was, to me, more than a personal grief. It was a heavy political loss for the Imperial cause which I had so much at heart. He had no sooner reached the summit of power than his health failed him. All that he might have done was left undone, for there was no one to take his place with the same dedication and the same clear-sighted purpose. His death was a tragedy that lives with me after long years.

The third of these friends was Richard Bedford Bennett. I was instantly attracted to him first as a young boy, and our friendship deepened as the years went on. It was fortified by a wide measure of political agreement. It was not unbroken, in contrast with my friendship with James Dunn and Bonar Law, but it was still a friendship which I greatly valued.

Both Bonar Law and Richard Bennett were political associates as well as personal friends, and both were victims of the irony of Fate. For they attained power only to lose it, through no fault or misjudgment of their own.

Bonar Law was broken by ill health. R. B. Bennett was broken by the Great Depression. He had absolutely no responsibility for that disaster. On the contrary, he made heroic efforts to mitigate its effects. But he was Prime Minister when the economic blizzard hit Canada and, in consequence, he became identified in the public mind with a poverty and wretchedness he had done nothing whatsoever to bring about. He was swept out of power at the general election of 1935, and never held office again. Any other politician would have suffered the same fate, but Canada could ill afford to lose the firm rule and wise guidance of R. B. Bennett.

James Dunn was a friend pure and simple. We were a long way apart in politics. He was a lifelong Liberal, and, as I have said, I was a follower of the Conservative Leader, Bonar Law. Nor did we have any business interests in common. Although his activities were many and varied, they never touched on mine.

But I knew him almost from my earliest years and we maintained a heartwarming companionship to the end. I greatly enjoyed his zest, his liveliness and his generosity of spirit. He left no mark on politics, nor did he want to, but he left an indelible mark on the economic life of Canada.

The fact that these three men were all from New Brunswick no doubt gave them a certain affinity, but the friendship I enjoyed with them had far stronger ties than a common origin.

Even so, there can be no doubt that the environment in which they grew up did much to mould their character and destiny.

Life was tough in New Brunswick in the last quarter of the last century. In the towns of the Province there was no electric light. The telephone was still a rare and novel instrument. There were no lavatories. There was no sewerage system. Drinking water had to be brought from a well. For fuel we depended on birch logs from the forest. Thus it was that the pump and the hand-saw were the portion of every boy in the Province, and of many a girl as well.

Social life was entirely home-made, for there were no meeting places except the church and the Sunday School. The best we could hope for was a snow-shoe party on a moonlight night in mid-winter or a Church Sunday School picnic on a sunny day in mid-summer.

The extremes of climate were a challenge to fortitude. There was a great heat in summer and intense cold in winter. The same extremes were to be found in the economic life of the Province in those days. There was either an acute shortage of labour for lumbering operations, or there were hard times and idle hands.

In these circumstances, family life demanded co-operation from all. Even the youngest had to take their share of the labours on the farm or chores about the house. These tasks ate into the time that the ambitious and enquiring youth could spend on study. Duty in the home must come first.

Indeed, study was not approved of, except for some severely practical purpose. There were no public libraries and the habit of general reading was not widespread. Reading for pure pleasure or to satisfy an unprofitable curiosity was not encouraged. There was no room for flights of fancy in a Province where life was real and grimly earnest.

In schools the teaching was good, but the buildings were inadequate and few of the homes could offer decent facilities for study. It was a constricting environment for a boy of imagination, ambition and vision. It was a simple world working on simple principles.

Even the administration of justice took on the tone of the community. Justice was rough, but it was honest. If the wrongdoer were found to have done wrong, he paid the penalty. The niceties of sophisticated law may not always have been preserved. But justice was done. The guilty were always punished and the innocent found protection.

That was the world into which James Dunn was born. It was not a world which agreed with his temperament or measured up to his ambitions. In contrast to the sober caution and careful thrift of New Brunswick, he developed into a man who lived more splendidly and lavishly than any other I have ever known.

In the days of his wealth and power, he rejected the meagre standards of New Brunswick —except for one thing. Like almost every boy in the Province, he had been bred on the Shorter Catechism. He was possibly unaware of it, but the Shorter Catechism was the greatest formative influence on his character and his career.

For the Shorter Catechism makes a bold virtue of getting on in the world. In other declarations of faith, the improvement of a man's material condition may be accepted as a permissible purpose in life. But in Calvinism it is enjoined and imposed upon the faithful. It is laid down as a duty.

In the questions and answers to the eighth commandment, the Shorter Catechism says that this commandment "requires the lawful procuring and furthering of the wealth and outward estate of ourselves and others." That is a positive injunction. Negatively, the Catechism forbids "Whatever doth or may unjustly hinder our own or our neighbour's wealth or outward estate."

James Dunn learned these words at the same time as he learned the multiplication tables.

He did not always conform to the faith of his fathers and he rejected the provincial life of New Brunswick at the close of the nineteenth century, but the words of the Catechism had sunk in. In his last years of great wealth and power, not even friendship would mollify him if he felt that his rights were being invaded. The man who denied his rights was hindering his wealth and was therefore a sinner. He would not have put it at that time in theological terms, but Calvinist

theology and John Knox's teaching had nevertheless made him what he was.

As his wealth grew, so did his expenditure on
what he called "gracious living". With his fleet
of cars, his airplanes, his fastidious and expensive
choice of clothing and food, he had journeyed
far from the austere and severely practical standards of New Brunswick. Perhaps he was even
seeking compensation for the deprivations of his
childhood and youth.

But Milton said that "New Presbyter is but
Old Priest writ large." Was "gracious living"
any more than "outward estate" writ large?

We do not escape easily from the pit whence
we were digged.

Mrs. Robert Dunn, mother of James. In 1881 she was housekeeper at Gowan Brae, Bathurst.

"Her love and sacrifice were fully rewarded by her grateful son."

James Dunn. At the age of seven.

"I ask what will the future be?"

Chapter 1

THURSDAY'S CHILD

I ask what will the Future be?
            —COATES

JAMES DUNN WAS born in Bathurst Village in the Province of New Brunswick, Canada. The year of his birth is not precisely known because at that time births, marriages and deaths in New Brunswick were registered in the church. The Presbyterian church in Bathurst, like all others in the Province, was built of wood. One day it caught fire and was burned to the ground. All the records were destroyed. Just when he was given the baptismal blessing is wrapped in impenetrable mystery. Possibly before the end of the year 1874 the minister, addressing himself to the infant in his mother's arms, said:

"The Lord bless thee and keep thee; the Lord make His face to shine upon thee, and be gracious unto thee; the Lord lift up His countenance upon thee, and give thee peace."

I have accepted the 29th of October, 1874 as James Dunn's birthday.

James Dunn's grandfather had come to Bathurst from Ireland. He was a builder of small boats and had two sons, Robert, who was James's

25

father, and William. They had a little shipyard on the eastern side of Bathurst Bay. They were humble people, with no importance, even locally. There is a photograph of his father which shows him to have been a very good-looking man with many of his son James's characteristic features. But it was his mother from whom James Dunn inherited his brains and enterprise.

Her maiden name was Eliza Jodrey. I remember her as a tall and handsome woman. She was well known to our family, for my father (Scottish minister) frequently preached at Bathurst.

When James was only a few months old, his mother was left a widow. Her husband fell into Bathurst Harbour in winter weather, trying to break up a jam of logs at the mouth of the river. He died of pneumonia when he was barely twenty-eight.

It was said that Mrs. Dunn mortgaged her little home and sold what furniture she did not need to help in bringing up her son. Her life was lonely and without much comfort, but her love and sacrifice were fully rewarded by her grateful son.

She had been a Morse Code instructor before marriage, travelling up and down the Intercolonial Railway, teaching young men and women to be train dispatchers. She took employment as a commercial telegraph operator in Bathurst. Her husband left one thousand dollars, but this she was determined to reserve for the education of her son. She entrusted it to her husband's brother to hold until the boy would be old enough to claim it for himself. Then she took up employment as housekeeper at Gowan Brae, home of the Ferguson family.

Like H. G. Wells, whose mother while housekeeper in a stately mansion in old England was permitted to give him food and shelter, so Mrs. Dunn was allowed to provide for her son at the home of the Ferguson family.

She was a prominent member of St. Luke's Presbyterian church in Bathurst and a deeply religious woman. She was also cautious and frugal.

When James began to make money, his first care was to shower her with every possible luxury. As soon as he could afford it, he built a fine home for her and presented her with a horse and carriage, and a groom to drive it. When motor cars came into general use, the horse and carriage gave way to an automobile with a chauffeur. He gave his mother six hundred dollars a month, but she cautiously banked half of that against a possible rainy day when James might have need of it.

He also insisted that she should have a hospital nurse as well as a housekeeper, but this was too much for a self-reliant woman. She thought the expense was quite unnecessary.

So, she did without the nurse. But whenever she heard that James was coming to Bathurst she borrowed two nurses from the hospital which her son had presented to the town. They stayed with her for the duration of his visit and then returned to their wards.

She died in 1918. By that time James was not possessed of great wealth, and he had no far-reaching power, but he was an important and prosperous man. She could look upon him with pride, and recall with happiness the love and devotion she had always so amply given him.

The brief inscription on the tombstone in the local cemetery—"Eliza A. Jodrey, wife of Robert H. Dunn, died 1918"—tells nothing of the bond of love between mother and son.

James Dunn and I spent much of our boyhood close together. Every summer my parents rented a cottage at Youghall Beach five miles from Bathurst. James also stayed at Youghall with the Armstrong family, relatives of the Dunns. Our cottage was small, primitive and over-crowded and living conditions were not comfort-able. But we had a wonderful time on the beauti-ful beach of the Baie de Chaleur. In fact when the weather was fine we were hardly ever indoors. We explored the beach looking for wrecks. When the tide went out we always hoped that the retreating sea would uncover a pirates' treasure, possibly a chest of gold.

When a storm blew up, we took refuge in a spruce grove where moss lay thick on the ground. We talked endlessly on many things, especially about boats, but I cannot remember that we ever talked about our future. I suspect that the absorb-ing present is enough for most boys.

It was always a happy holiday time but there was one cloud upon our joy. That was the Sabbath. Mrs. Dunn was such a strict Sabbatarian that she would not allow James to play games or even to whittle sticks on the Seventh Day. My father held an open air service, which James attended sometimes and myself always. But we were not voluntary attenders. We were conscripts.

One day on the road to Youghall I met with an accident. I fell under a mowing machine that was being pulled along by a waggon. I, with some other boys, was holding on to the shaft of the machine. I slipped and a wheel ran over my head.

After a brief coma I recovered and was none the worse. Indeed, James claimed that I was much the better. He always maintained that I had been a stupid boy before I went under the wheel and became a clever boy afterwards. I did much to spread the story, but I did not fail to remind him that he also had hold of a carriage shaft that made him what he was. I was referring to the mother to whom he owed so much.

In adult life we sometimes went back to Bathurst to revisit the scenes of our boyhood. I remember once sitting with him on the beach and asking: "Why not reconstruct the old family shipyard and build pleasure boats and racing yachts for the market in Montreal?"

He shook his head. "Wooden boats are finished," he said. "The ships of metal, plastics

and fibre will replace the old tubs. Wooden
boats grow old as men grow old, until the day
comes when they are no longer freshly painted
every Spring, but left up on the banks to fall into
decay. And there they rest in the warm sunshine
of retirement."

James would never have anything to do with
decay and nothing to do with retirement either.
He would often quote Tim Healy's advice:
"Don't resign. Wait until you're sacked." He
would improve on that, saying: "Don't retire.
Wait until you're dead."

At school James proved an apt and conscien-
tious pupil. James McIntosh, the headmaster of
St. Luke's School, Bathurst Village, thought well
of him and encouraged him. James always remembered and made much of a prize he won. It
was a book inscribed: "To Jimmie Dunn, Highest
marks for lessons and conduct in his class, St.
Luke's School Bathurst, 1881."

The book was an adventure story, *Paul Howard's Captivity; and how he escaped*. James
certainly escaped from the captivity of limited
opportunity in his native Bathurst.

He merited no prizes for conduct outside of
school. The boys of the district were a boisterous
lot. There was no vice in them, but they were
rough and ready and everyone had to fight his
own corner. At the foot of the hill on the
Bathurst Road stood a pump with a large oblong
wooden box, not unlike an open coffin, filled
with water. This was the horse trough. It was

also the place where arguments were settled with fists between young lads. Sometimes James won these arguments and sometimes he lost, for his spirit was always far greater than his strength. But he never accepted a defeat as final. Always the last round had to be his.

James was a stout athlete. He would run round Bathurst Basin, a distance of three miles, in his bare feet, to keep himself in condition.

This barefoot habit remained with him all through his life.

Though slender he was wiry. He was an exceedingly good-looking boy with an interesting though intense countenance. His well-shaped head, jutting jaw and direct gaze marked him as a young man of distinction.

He kept his spare figure to the end.

He was lively, high-spirited and quick-tempered. He also showed a strong acquisitive instinct from an early age. If there was a good seat vacant in a buggy, James was the first to nip in. There was no nonsense about politely offering it to someone else. He wanted the best that was to be got.

I did not always appreciate his determination to get his own way. Some of us youngsters had formed an exclusive little club of our own called the Cypress Club. This owed its name to the fact that we were imaginative and maybe we had been talking about the Far East where we thought cypress trees grew.

We would not admit James nor my eldest

brother Traven Aitken, for, besides being older than the rest of us, they were bigger and stronger and altogether too much for us to control. And we did not want to be dominated by them in our own club.

But they would not allow themselves to be black-balled by boys smaller than themselves. They therefore besieged our little fortress. We barricaded the door so that it was impossible to break it down. But we had reckoned without the ingenuity of James Dunn. He abandoned any notion of battering his way in, and came through the transom over the door. This act was characteristic. He often found a way round when obstacles confronted him. Although in this siege engagement we were on opposite sides, James was as a rule my friend and protector in youthful scrapes.

There came a time when the serious business of life had to be faced. School could do no more for James. He had set his heart on a university course, but that required money. James set out to claim from his uncle the thousand dollars that were his due.

His uncle had moved to the Middle West of the United States where he had set up in the timber business. Over the years he did not often communicate with his brother's widow or her son. James set out to seek him at his last known address.

He travelled by train to the end of the line and then hired a farmer with a horse and buckboard to carry him the rest of the way. It took some time to reach the remote spot where the uncle was carrying on his lumbering business, and there was no comfort when he got there. The money was gone.

The young lad reported to his mother: "My uncle said that he had invested the money and lost it."

Thus James's first experience of adult money transactions was a betrayal of trust. It was not to be his last. Long afterwards, when he was soaring high in the world of finance, wealthy, courted and admired, another betrayal of trust on a far greater scale brought him, without warning, face to face with ruin and the destruction of his whole brilliant career.

Chapter 2

SMALL POTATOES

"How are your potatoes?
Very small.
How do you eat them?
Skins and all!"

—New Brunswick Folk Song

Although his journey in search of his lost thousand dollars was the first adventure of James Dunn into the outside world, he had more knowledge of life and its problems than most other young boys.

No one comes closer to the heart of the realities of human life than a doctor, especially a doctor with a country practice. James Dunn had become the protégé of just such a man.

In the village of Bathurst, Dr. Gideon Duncan, the local physician and surgeon, carried on an extensive horse-and-buggy practice in town and country.

James Dunn, who had been brought into the world with the doctor's help, became in turn the doctor's helper. Frequently, he "took the reins" as the doctor's old grey mare carried them both on the rounds of patients through village streets and country roads.

The doctor, who was also an elder at St. Luke's Presbyterian Church, showed a great and lively interest in the village school and its pupils. Between "The Old Doctor", as he was called, and "The Little Lad", as Dunn was nicknamed because of his slight build, there sprang into being that rare and warm bond of friendship that can only develop between the very young and the very old.

Dr. Duncan always carried with him a book on botany, for he had great hopes of finding some new, undiscovered plant or flower.

He never found the flower he sought, but he planted seeds of value in young Dunn's mind. He inspired him with his own love of nature and the freedom of the open air. He taught him compassion and the joy of helping others.

Dunn would even assist at operations, which the old doctor would perform on the kitchen table in his patient's home.

Dunn's part on these occasions was to administer chloroform on a pad, and to hand the doctor the instruments as he needed them.

Years afterwards, he would tell stories about these early days and add that he could still hear the doctor say: "Damn it, Jim, do you want to *kill* the patient?" when he became too liberal with the chloroform.

As time went on and Dunn grew prosperous, he was generous to the old man and saw he

lacked for nothing in his decline. After the good
doctor died, full of years, his home Ellerslie
was taken over by James and turned into a cottage hospital. It was a good deed of much benefit
to a community sorely in need of a medical
centre.

The influence of Dr. Gideon Duncan was considerable in his own time and survived his death
in the conduct of James Dunn, who never failed
in sympathy for those in pain or misery. He was
always attentive to his bedridden companions,
and in the midst of his heavy business commitments he would turn aside to visit the hospital
or the home, bringing comfort always and assistance very often.

He was also genuinely interested in the people
with whom he worked, and who worked for him.
He felt a deep and real responsibility for them.
He helped many employees who came to him in
need—or whose need was brought to his notice.

When he became Chairman and President of
the famous Algoma Steel Works in 1935 he took
particular interest in the development of deposits
of iron ore.

The Helen Mine was the centre of these operations. One day, while Dunn was conferring with
his directors in his private railway carriage, the
mine doctor entered and, without interrupting
the meeting, asked Dr. Greig (who was Dunn's
personal physician) to look at one of his patients.

Presently the two doctors returned. George
MacLeod, Vice-President and general manager

of Algoma Ore Properties (a subsidiary of the Algoma Steel Company), asked Greig what was wrong. The doctor explained that a patient had damaged the structure of his leg playing baseball. By some serious and unexpected complication he was likely to lose his leg, and possibly his life, unless he could be treated very quickly at the Toronto General Hospital.

This treatment would be long, and would cost more than the man could afford. There thus seemed little hope of saving that broken leg.

All this while, James Dunn was apparently engaged in serious conversation with his directors. No one thought he could have heard what the doctor said. However, he turned and asked whether the patient was one of his employees.

George MacLeod replied that he was, but as he had not been injured on duty he was not covered by Workmen's Compensation.

Dunn asked Dr. Greig how much the necessary treatment would cost. The doctor replied that at the very least it would be several thousand dollars. Dunn nodded and turned to his secretary.

"See that this man is taken to Toronto, and send the bill to me personally," he said.

That workman, whom Dunn had never even met, was operated on with success. After three months in hospital at Dunn's expense, he returned to the mine entirely cured, and was still on the Algoma staff when James died.

I could fill a book full of stories about the concern and compassion James Dunn showed to

those in distress, and of the assistance that
flowed from the understanding heart of this
extraordinary man. And as Bunyan wrote of
another great spirit in Pilgrim's Progress: "The
more he cast away, the more he had."

Dunn had come to know human suffering and
helpless misery from his experience with Dr.
Gideon Duncan, among that good doctor's patients at Bathurst Village, and throughout the
vast though sparsely populated countryside.

The knowledge never left him. He declared to
me once that a career in the medical profession
had tempted him in his youth. But he said Doctor Duncan did not get paid for most of his work.
His total income was so small that James's idea
of "gracious living" would not be reconciled
with a country doctor's practice and what it
would yield.

When James's schooldays were over, he gave
up the Saturday-Sunday holiday drive behind the
doctor's old grey mare, and looked for work with
a reasonable money reward and hope for better
things to come.

Jobs were hard to find in New Brunswick towards the end of the last century. We had to
take what was going. Most of us had several tries
before we settled down. James was no exception.

With his mother he set out for Lynn, Massa-
chusetts, U.S.A., where members of their family
lived.

James looked for work. He was employed as
a sales clerk in a large store. His reward was

small and his employer's demands were big. So
James, in a moment of rebellious conduct, lost
his job and his pittance.

He found work winding armatures for dyna-
mos in the Thomson-Houston plant. His pay
was twelve dollars a week.

Although he was working a full day of labour
with his hands, he still maintained his interest in
boxing and physical fitness. One day, in a fair-
ground booth, he won a boxing prize of ten
dollars.

This apparently chance happening changed the
entire course of his life. For had James Dunn not
been small and slight, he might not have been so
eager to prove his worth against bigger men in
the boxing ring. And had he not done so, then
he would never have won this prize which his
talent and energy multiplied a millionfold.

With part of this money he bought a ticket
for a lecture being given locally by a so-called
Professor, named Loisette, who was speaking
on memory, and how to improve it.

His discourse so impressed Dunn—whose own
memory was already remarkable—that the boy
enrolled for a course of three lectures.

The Professor noticed this young, earnest fellow with the prodigious memory listening in-
tently to what he had to say, and he took a liking
to him. They had many conversations. Finally,
the Professor hired him as an advance agent to
go before him when he was on tour to engage
halls for his lectures.

Dunn also had to make sure that proper notices and advertisements about the Professor and his wife—"Madame"—appeared in the local newspapers and elsewhere.

He acquitted himself admirably and the Professor and his wife took a friendly interest in him.

Now the Professor was exceedingly tall and broad and of a tremendous weight. On two occasions, while staying at hotels, chairs collapsed under him. The managements added to their bills charges for damage to furniture. James, who was responsible for settlement of all accounts, declared to the hotels that the chairs were faulty. He made such a fuss over the physical disabilities the Professor had sustained, even claiming compensation, that the charges for ruined chairs were cancelled.

Loisette and his wife were so impressed by the persuasive qualities of James that they decided to take him with them to England where it was possible more chairs might fall under the heavyweight Professor.

James's argumentative capacity might save many a charge, just or otherwise.

They set sail in the *Campania* from New York for Liverpool on Saturday, November 17, 1894.

Dunn was naturally very excited at the prospect before him. It was indeed a challenge and a joy. Here he was, just twenty and sailing for London, the centre of all worlds—cultural, political, and financial.

James Dunn at Dunn's Camp

"The common sea, the air, the skies,
To him are opening Paradise."

erkley, Leatherhead, House Party. 1921. *Left to right*: Colonial Secretary Winston Churchill, Mrs. Fitzgerald, Prime nister Lloyd George, G. H. M. Cartwright, Lady Eleanor Smith, Randolph Lycett, James Dunn and Beaverbrook.

He wrote his impressions to his mother and grandmother, and even at such a time of excitement he sent one dollar to each of them—two dollars which took some saving, for the Professor did not pay him a regular wage.

To his mother he wrote an account of the sea journey: "We are on the largest and finest vessel afloat. She is now steaming about $22\frac{1}{2}$ knots an hour or nearly 25 miles. Faster than the ordinary railway train and without apparently any difficulty. We are saloon passengers and have the best accommodation in every respect. We eat here five times daily."

On the Sunday morning he rose at 7.30, "had a cold salt bath and something to eat and drink.

"I talked with the purser and walked about until 10.30 when I attended Divine Service," he wrote. "This is an English ship and we had their service. The vessel is rolling somewhat and it is hard to stand straight in singing."

One dollar was enclosed and he declared, "I am afraid to send more in an unregistered letter."

He risked another dollar in his short and fascinating letter to his grandmother:

"Dear Grandma,

"I will write you a long letter on the steamer and mail it from London. I am not sick [seasick].

"God bless and keep you both till I see you again.

"I enclose you a dollar also.

Your loving grandson
J. H. DUNN."

Two dollars from his meagre income was surely the limit of his resources and an interesting example of his generous spirit even in his early years.

By November 29 the voyage was over. He wrote to his mother and grandmother: "Well, I'm in London, we came straight through from Liverpool as soon as we landed, by train, an English train and very little I think of their trains and many other things. After much difficulty we succeeded in getting a Handsome to carry us from the Depot to the Hotel (The Grand).

"Madame had been several times in Europe but never in England before, and London was new to her as well as to me.

"It was one o'clock in the morning and London was asleep when we drove through it the first time. Next morning when I awoke, or rather next afternoon (it was 1 p.m.) the Professor and Madame were out so I started out to see some of the Metropolis.

"On our way from Liverpool I heard an Englishman exclaim—'dear old dirty London'—and I never heard greater truth than the latter part of his phrase, for London is the dirtiest city I have ever seen. Smoke and fog, fog and smoke, while between them both I have not yet seen the sun. It is very warm here, no appearance of snow or frost but still it is dank and the air is heavy.

"I am boarding in a private hotel on Norfolk

Street in a house owned by the Duke and kept
by a very nice lady."

"Everything in London is of the same grey
colour," he wrote. "Taking London as I have
seen it and all its people, I would rather live in
America with Americans or in Canada with Canadians than remain here, but perhaps it is not a
fair sample of England. If I am a judge, London
is just a little behind New York or Boston,
though, of course, much larger."

On his first visit to London, although he was
critical of England and the English, there is no
doubt that his ambition was sharpened. Stimu-
lated by his experience, he determined to make
an immediate success. He meant to have power
and to live splendidly. He must now turn to the
study of law, for which Canada afforded opportunities that he could not find in England.

He therefore returned home in the *R.M.S.
Pomerania.*

While he was abroad, my brothers and I had
missed him greatly. With admiration and envy
we had heard accounts of his letters from England. Then one day word came to us that he was
on his way back to Bathurst Village.

Would he come home to us like the prodigal
son or in a cloud of glory? Filled with curiosity,
I decided to meet him at the railway station. As
he stepped down from the train, all uncertainties
were dispelled.

Although he was travelling second class, he
was magnificently dressed with every appearance

of abounding prosperity. He carried a gold-topped cane and wore a wonderfully-cut city suit and the most beautiful patent leather boots I had ever seen.

I was wearing what were called shoe-packs, a sort of moccasin, heavily oiled to keep out the snow and the slush. They looked crude and homely indeed alongside the shoes of my friend James Dunn.

How I admired those glittering, pointed boots of his, so dazzling with their shine that I wished with all my heart to own such a pair myself! Indeed, I asked him at the station whether he would exchange his shoes for my moccasins. He rejected my proposal with a certain touch of patronage.

There was no transportation in Bathurst in those days. Even if there had been a sleigh available, we could not have afforded to hire it. So we set off on foot over Bathurst Bridge on the way to his home. As we walked, his beautiful patent leather boots began to disintegrate in the snow, while my moccasins or shoe-packs stood up splendidly.

Even in his youth, James was given to picturesque language. He declared vigorously that his boots were of "fraudulent durability".

I admired his words, even though his boots failed to hold any further interest for me.

After more than half a century had passed, his wife made me the present of a pair of stout snow-shoes. And James wrote to me: "This winter we might walk across the bridge in zero weather going North to the village. This task will remind us of that bitter, cold day sixty years ago when I offered at journey's end to exchange my patent leather for your shoe-packs."

We did return to Bathurst quite often, and for the last time shortly before he died. It was not in the midst of winter but while summer still tarried on the beaches of the Baie de Chaleur. James described the purpose of our visit.

"Looking for an old log," he said, "where we shared one lunch between two hungry boys."

We were not really hungry in those early days. But money was scarce. And work was not plentiful.

The young James Dunn, on returning from his jaunt to London, took up employment in the office of George Gilbert, a local lawyer. He was articled as a law student.

James thought he was fortunate in finding a place so soon. But, as matters turned out, it was also great good fortune for Mr. Gilbert when James Dunn came to him as a student.

Dunn never forgot his employer, and when he became prosperous, he also became a guardian angel to the older man.

It was indeed a most rewarding and stimulating experience to see these two men together in their latter days. For Gilbert always remained the master, although Dunn supplied the cash. Dunn treated the old man with such respect and

consideration that Gilbert still felt he was the
teacher, and Dunn remained the boy who had
come to his office nearly sixty years before.

The hospital which James provided for the
citizens of Bathurst was, like the Presbyterian
Church, built of wood. It was after 1950 that
fire destroyed it. James proposed a plan of reconstruction. The community was asked to provide one dollar for every two from James himself. But a condition was attached to this generous
plan. Mr. Gilbert, who had been Chairman
throughout the life of the old hospital, must be
confirmed in office. Local opinion was opposed
to this choice because of Gilbert's age and in-
firmities. The conflict between James and his
opponents was never resolved. Bathurst still
waits for another benefactor and also another
hospital.

Gilbert outlived his patron. He died in December 1957, at the age of 90.

One day, James Dunn went on some legal er-
rand to Chatham, a town about 40 miles from
Bathurst, where I was an articled student typing
on an ancient machine with stickit keys in a back
room in the law office of Tweedie & Bennett. I
think that this would be the first time that Dunn
and R. B. Bennett met.

It has always been gratifying to me that despite several years' difference in our ages—Dunn
was five years older than I, and Bennett nine
years my senior—we all kept in close touch with
one another. And we all achieved some of our

ambitions, although our lives followed quite different courses.

Sir James Dunn, Bart., reached a position of leadership in Canadian industry.

Bennett was Canada's Prime Minister from 1930 to 1935 and from 1941 a Member of the House of Lords.

Bennett died a few days before his 77th birthday; Dunn lived to be 81; and I am now eighty-two.

Very early in their association, George Gilbert realised that his young student had unusual promise, and advised him to go to the Law School at Dalhousie University, Halifax, Nova Scotia.

Dunn therefore enrolled as a law student.

In later years, he liked to talk of his student days at Dalhousie, when he did not have enough money to take a degree in the arts and barely enough to study law.

But he paid his way as he went along, working in holidays as a deck-hand aboard a Halifax tug-boat, and for the Halifax Electric Tramway Company.

Years afterwards, he was to become a Governor of Dalhousie University, but as a student he lodged in a room in Spring Garden Road with two other students from St. Francis Xavier University. Possibly he paid two dollars weekly for his bed and board.

James Dunn, who came to own the most magnificent wine cellar in all Canada, whose personal valet would preside over every meal that was cooked for him, even in the world's most exclusive hotels, lived frugally as a student. His evening meal was a plate of beans with a little molasses and a glass of water.

But the three young students livened their evenings with spirited debates on the issues of the day. Dunn was the leader among them and, as always, a remarkable conversationalist and a clever story-teller.

His class-mates remember him not so much as a man of academic mind, but as a vigorous debater and the most rebellious questioner of his lecturers.

Once, when Professor Benjamin ("Benny") Russell, later Chief Justice of Nova Scotia, gave some legal interpretation in the classroom concerning property law, Dunn jumped to his feet.

"Lord Eldon," he declared, *"with whom I agree*, has a different opinion!"

Needless to say, this different opinion of Dunn's—and Lord Eldon's—carried the day.

James also cut a fine figure on the curling rink and was very popular with the curling community. He could "sweep it up" with considerable vigour and had some understanding of the geometrical character of the game.

Once he broke his shoulder during an unusually fierce rugger match—a game he also enjoyed—and one of his colleagues wrote this verse about him:

"There's Jamie Dunn, Q.C.
Who lately broke his shoulder.
In days of yore his name was Did
But now he's getting bolder.
He's fond of giving Benny* points,
And gives them free at that.
Some day I fear his head may be
Much bigger than his hat."

In fact, his hat was always big.

Continually hard pressed for money, Dunn became assistant librarian in his spare time so that he could earn $50. In his third year, needing to earn still more in order to carry on, he walked into the office of a man who was to exert a singular influence upon his career—Benjamin Franklin Pearson—and asked for work.

He saw Mr. W. H. Covert, Pearson's partner, and explained his predicament to him. As a third-year man, Dunn believed that if he worked he would be paid something, and he was certainly willing to work.

Mr. Covert recalled that "as the head of my firm and close friend, B. F. Pearson, had at that time crowded us with work, I readily agreed.

"Jimmy Dunn—as we then called him—took hold so amazingly that he aroused the interest of Mr. Pearson, and after Dunn graduated from Dalhousie and was admitted to the Bar, Pearson told a group, headed by Mr. Greenshields, a leading lawyer in Montreal, that here was a singularly able young man."

---

* Professor Benjamin Russell.

Fifty years later, Covert's nephew moved that this same singularly able man should become Honorary President of Dalhousie Alumni Association in succession to our friend the late Lord Bennett.

In the University magazine, the *Dalhousie Gazette*, of November 13, 1896, an account appeared of a mock parliament in which "The Hon. J. H. Dunn" was aptly chosen as "Minister of Finance". Dunn certainly left a mark on the student community and under the heading: "Our Graduates, 1898", in the issue of the *Gazette* dated October 26, 1898, there appeared a brief biography of him.

"James Hamet Dunn! He was a peculiar fellow; what pen can do him justice? He came amongst us breathing out threatenings and slaughter. No person ever had to ask twice for his opinion —

"Dunn was also an orator. With marvellous combinations of words and resistless logic he enthused and convinced his audience; his very look carried consternation to the hearts of his opponents. In his senior year 'Jimmie' became 'Mister'.

"The office-boy was ordered to call him 'Mr. Dunn'—and all others were expected to speak of him likewise."

On March 17, 1898, when he was 24, Dunn passed his final examinations and at once informed his mother of this good news.

"My darling Mother," he wrote on notepaper of the Halifax Tramway Company, "My examinations are all over and I am all through, having passed in every subject.

"I will get my degree in April and be admitted to the Nova Scotia Bar in the coming fall.

"Of course, I feel quite elated in a way to know that I am through in everything and that my college days are over and that I am a successful graduate of Dalhousie—more so, Mother, because I owe it to myself directly, and indirectly to you, and that means I owe it all to you because you, when I was a child, and all through my life, as I grew older, fostered my pride and my ambition and I resolved I would be somebody, even if my Uncle and guardian did squander my money and leave me pretty much on my own resources.

"I spent part of the evening (up to nine o'clock) at Mrs. Pearson's* and then I came down to the office to write to you the result of my exams. It is quite late and I am going home and to bed, for lately I have been plugging late and need some rest.

"They have just finished cleaning my room at the house and old Miss Tupper has been very kind to me, she has swiftly made a little palace of it—new curtains and wallpaper and my armchair covered and everything looking lovely."

Miss Tupper had been his landlady in Halifax; it was typical that he remembered her little kindnesses to him all her life.

---

* Wife of B. F. Pearson.

James Dunn's graduation marks were high. Dr. Richard C. Weldon, the Dean of the Law Faculty of Dalhousie, wrote a very warm reference about him in the year before he took his finals.

"This certifies that James H. Dunn is a student in the Dalhousie Law School, having attended lectures during two years. That so far he has taken the highest rank of the students of his class at the Sessional Examination, that he has been Assistant Librarian in the Law School during the present year.

"He will be found to possess excellent ability and will be, I believe, energetic and faithful in the discharge of duties assigned to him."

Dr. Weldon was a remarkable man who did not give his praise lightly. He had founded the Law Faculty at Dalhousie, and was its first Dean, a position he held for many years.

Weldon often praised Dunn's wisdom and his character. Shortly before he died, Dunn told a classmate of his, the Hon. Charles J. Burchell, that he attributed much of his success in life, not only as a lawyer, but as a man, to what he called "the wholesome influence and guidance of Dr. Weldon".

In the momentous years ahead, James Dunn certainly lived up to his Dean's faith in him.

On September 14, he was admitted and enrolled as a Barrister, Solicitor and Attorney of the Supreme Court of Nova Scotia.

He went to work full-time for Pearson and

Covert. I imagine that he was not paid very much, probably only a pittance. He took a great fancy to Pearson's pretty daughter, though nothing came of this attraction.

Pearson was a strong and generous character, an outstanding leader of Municipal and Provincial activity in Nova Scotia. He might be described as a lawyer-promoter—a good promoter who brought prosperity to the city and to the countryside.

He was never a greedy man—as are so many promoters, and especially lawyer-promoters— but, on the contrary, he was in everything open-handed and kindly. He had sympathy for the hopes and aspirations of youth and encouraged them in James Dunn and in others.

In fact, Dunn's meeting with Pearson was a pivotal point in his advancement.

B. F. Pearson was identified with a project for building a railway from Edmonton, Alberta, to the Great Slave Lake territory in the North.

He recommended Dunn to set up in the practice of law in Alberta, with a retainer to look after the interests of the proposed railway project. Dunn went to Edmonton, Alberta, where he practised law with another young man named Cross, who afterwards became Attorney General of the Province.

Dunn did not stay long in the West, for the railway remained no more than a vision. There just was not enough money available at that time to build it.

I was in Edmonton while Dunn was there, engaged on a minor commercial undertaking of my own, sending shipments of produce to the Crow's Nest Pass.

We two talked incessantly and always at night. I argued that the West was the land of opportunity. Patience would be rewarded.

Dunn did not agree with this opinion. He held that the East had greater possibilities of swifter development and earlier growth.

"The West must pay tribute to the East," was how he put it. "And I'm off to the East where I can collect tribute."

As usual with him, he was immediately ready to back his judgment with hard and definite action.

He went East. And so did I.

But, of course, while the East to me meant New Brunswick, the East to Dunn meant the biggest city in the whole of the Dominion, where he could find the largest population, the greatest concentration of wealth and the best chance of success on a grand scale.

He went to Montreal.

There he was admitted to the Bar, and on the recommendation of Pearson of Halifax he was given employment by the Greenshields firm of lawyers. That might well have been his permanent resting place had not immediate opportunity arisen for him to show not only his business and intellectual acumen, but also his very considerable physical courage and audacity.

The principal of the firm, the late J. M. Greenshields, Q.C., acted as Counsel for the Montreal
Cotton Company at Valleyfield, P.Q., where the
operators were on strike.

A very serious and explosive situation prevailed at the plant. It involved "reading the Riot
Act" and calling out the Militia to maintain
order among the strikers, who were threatening
violent action.

James Dunn was sent by his firm to the scene.
He met and calmed an angry mob of strikers
engaging in sabotage. More than that and against
all expectation, he negotiated a swift and satisfactory settlement of the strike.

When it was all over, Greenshields was suffi-
ciently impressed to promote Dunn from employee to junior partner in the firm.

Thus, at only 26, James Dunn was already
recognized as a promising young man destined
to do well in his profession.

But his restless eyes were seeking new and
more tempting horizons, beyond the world of
law. He wanted to deal in millions, to hammer
out his dreams on the ringing anvil of achievement.

Chapter 3

LOVE AND LONDON

Dame Nature gave him comeliness and health,
And Fortune (for a passport) gave him wealth.
                                                                    —HARTE

THEN, JAMES DUNN, the junior partner in the important law firm of Greenshields, Henniker and Dunn, fell in love.

The girl of his choice was Gertrude Price, the daughter of Herbert Molesworth Price, a lumber man in a big way of business in Quebec.

Dunn was married on August 28, 1901, and the general feeling among his friends was that he had made a very good choice.

Gertrude Price came from a family of importance and wealth, and all of us who knew James intimately felt that, as a rising young lawyer, he had extended his influence and associations.

His marriage certainly began very well. He and his wife made their home in Montreal. Five children were to be born. The eldest, Mona, was born in 1902. Philip was born in 1905, Kathleen two years later, Joan in 1908 and Bridget in 1919.

Very soon it was apparent that the restless energy of James Dunn could not be satisfied with a career in the practice of law. He had qualified as a lawyer only because he believed that he would then hold a key to wealth. All large financial deals needed lawyers to draw up contracts and to approve agreements. But he was determined to be the principal in making contracts and agreements. Others would be employed to draw up the documents. James Dunn decided to move on.

He satisfied his desire for action by plunging into the whirlpool of Canadian finance. Borrowing $20,000 from his father-in-law, Mr. Herbert Price, he bought a seat on the Montreal Stock Exchange, and on August 26, 1902, he became a member.

His early experiences on the Stock Exchange were not at all successful. James was for the moment carried away by the apparent ease and facility with which he could make money by buying and selling shares. He joined with the sons of two wealthy Montreal families in a project known as the "Kindergarten Pool", which they believed would make their fortunes.

They bought heavily into the shares of Dominion Steel and then proceeded to bid up the price. For a time they showed a handsome paper profit.

But lasting wealth is not made so easily. An experienced market operator, Rudolphe Forget, had been selling his considerable holdings in the same shares as they rose in value. Suddenly he attacked the price of the stock by heavy short sales, and when Dunn and his friends tried to liquidate they found that their market had melted away.

The members of the "Kindergarten Pool" were in difficulties. Powerful and wealthy James Ross came to the rescue. But instead of making large profits, the group had suffered substantial losses.

However, Dunn learned from this early escapade that there can be no quick, easy way to financial success. He told me of his decision to restrain his spirit of adventure in future and to stick to orthodox finance.

His correspondent in New York was the firm of Laidlaw & Company. He used their headquarters when he visited the financial capital of the United States. He was often spoken of by old employees of the Laidlaw office because of his excellent taste in clothes. He wore a bowler hat and he always carried a cane and smoked Bock Twist cigars. This made a very considerable impression upon the partners in New York.

In Montreal at this time a good deal of arbitrage went on; brokers would take advantage of varying prices of stocks and shares in other markets. They would buy a stock in Montreal, for instance, and sell it in New York, or the other way about. James Dunn became a brilliant operator in arbitrage, which made him a steady income.

But his first real money in his new career was made by dealing in Mexican securities. He met an American engineer and promoter named

F. S. Pearson, who must not be confused with
B. F. Pearson, the lawyer-promoter of Halifax,
Nova Scotia.

F. S. Pearson was an extraordinary promoter
of companies. There seemed no end to his activities. When Dunn met him, Pearson was
seeking money in Canada to finance lighting
companies in Mexico, tramways in Rio de
Janeiro and various other public utility enterprises in the South.

James undertook to join in marketing securities of these companies. He would pay par value
for bonds, receiving free an equal par value in
bonus shares. He then resold the bonds with half
his bonus shares to investors. His profits therefore depended on the value of the bonus remaining in his hands, which he sold separately on the
Stock Exchange to speculative buyers. These
profits were considerable.

All this while, Dunn was associated with Mc-
Kay Edgar, a member of the Stock Exchange.
There is a contemporary account of a conversation between Edgar and Robert Hickson, who
also was a member of the Montreal Stock Exchange. At this time I was in business in Halifax,
Nova Scotia.

"Bob," said Edgar one day, "I see you've sold
some Mexican bonds."

"That's quite right, Mike," Hickson agreed.

"Well," Edgar continued, "there's a fellow
in Halifax, named Aitken, who's going short on
these bonds, and if you are selling for him, be

careful, as Jimmy Dunn and I are going to give him a hell of a squeeze!"

As a matter of fact, Hickson was selling for a trust company and not for me. And there was no squeeze.

One evening James invited me to attend a banquet (as it was called) in Montreal at a downtown club. The dinner was in honour of F. S. Pearson. Nearly all the young financiers, the rising stockbrokers, and the thrusting promoters in the East were there, attracted by the certainty of good food, good drink and the probability of some fun.

The object of the banquet, of course, was to stimulate public interest in Pearson's enterprises and to sell more securities.

Pearson made a speech about the wonderful prospect of dazzling profits from water turned into electricity. Then came a flow of speeches when guests spoke well of their host and of Mr. Pearson and his "safe and profitable" output of bonds and shares in his many projects.

Then, at last, our host, James Dunn, rose to speak.

"I must thank Mr. Pearson for much," he began. "I thank him for all these excellent projects he brings to our market which extend and develop it. He is indeed a most useful and admirable patron of the Montreal Stock Exchange."

He went on his way, naming all the various benefits that Pearson was supposed to have conferred upon the financial community.

Then he added, almost casually: "And for myself, I must also thank him. *I* must thank him for a fortune that now amounts to $200,000!"

At this we all set up yells and shouts of laughter and derision, for we did not believe him.

Next day he proved to W. D. Ross and me with some indignation that the net market value of his assets in fact exceeded $200,000. We were convinced.

In 1905 he decided to invade London and make a market there for Pearson's securities. He reminded me of his advice in the West to the effect that we should both go East and make money. Now he said we should go further East and make more money. However, I had decided to move to Montreal. It was in the next year that I bought control of the Montreal Trust Company for $360,000. Thus I lost touch with him for a time.

James Dunn's branch office in the heart of the City of London was at 85 London Wall. He continued to operate in Montreal under the name of J. H. Dunn & Company, as a member of the Montreal Stock Exchange.

Two years later, in 1907, when James was 32, his London office became his principal centre and in time Coombe Hill, Kingston, his ordinary residence.

He terminated his connection with the Montreal stockbroking firm, transferring his Stock Exchange seat, some assets and his goodwill to his partner, Victor Gray, for a promise to pay

$57,000 with interest at 6 per cent. But he did not require Gray to relinquish the firm's name of J. H. Dunn and Company.

It was in the next year, in the summer, that Dunn arrived in Montreal from New York on the night train. Within the hour Victor Gray committed suicide. Neglect of business opportunities and foolish speculation in an attempt to retrieve his fortunes resulted in the inevitable collapse.

Although the partnership had been dissolved in 1907 the name of Dunn remained. James therefore hurried to the office and before nightfall he made a statement that Gray's liabilities would be met in full and forthwith. And they were.

He acknowledged his responsibility for the credit Gray had obtained. His good name was at stake. And he was not without some reward for his altruistic decision.

Amongst the letters he received I quote the following from one of the beneficiaries:

> "GRAND TRUNK RAILWAY SYSTEM
> St. Hyacinthe, Que.
> April 15th 1909

"My dear Mr. Dunn,

"I wanted to write to you long before this, but I had some difficulty in obtaining your address and hence my apparent dilatoriness.

Mr. N. K. Lafleur* of Montreal some weeks

---

* Name almost indecipherable

ago remitted me your cheque for $2,000.00, making a total of $4,000.00 received from you to cover my loss through Mr. Gray's death last July. I wish to express to you my most sincere gratitude for your extreme kindness and generosity towards me in that unfortunate instance Mr. Dunn.—I understand your position quite well and I am aware that, besides sustaining a heavy personal loss, that there was absolutely nothing binding you to any obligations towards me; and I realize to what extent this fact makes your action tangibly generous and broad.

"I am now in position to make up my loss, and, in time, I hope to be able to remit at least a part of the sum you have disbursed to assist me.

"Thanking you again and wishing you prosperity and happiness, I beg to be

Yours respectfully & gratefully
R. E. CODERRE"

In London James took into partnership one Charles Louis Fischer, a Swiss national, and the firm of Messrs. Dunn, Fischer & Company soon became a well-known merchant banking house in the City. They occupied the greater part of a large building at 41 Threadneedle Street, within a few yards of the Bank of England and the London Stock Exchange.

Their staff was international. They employed French, Germans, Swiss and Italians, for their firm had ramifications over most of Europe and did business in many cities on the Continent.

A senior colleague of Dunn's in these early days was Paul Freytag, who belonged to a distinguished German family. Through his connections, he brought considerable German business to the firm. There were many deals with Hugo Stinnes, a wealthy German, who was concerned directly or indirectly in enterprises of importance in his own country.

In 1909 Dunn was appointed Agent in London for the Government of Alberta. Altogether, he was succeeding in a most astonishing way.

Meanwhile, Mr. Pearson, the promoter of South American public utilities, had also set up an office in London near Dunn, Fischer & Company. Dunn and Pearson worked as closely as ever they had done in Canada.

They were professionally and personally complementary to each other and had that rare gift of inspiring the investing public with their own enthusiasm for whatever project engaged their attention.

Both were endowed with strength of character, foresight and a physical endurance that was quite remarkable. When embarking upon some new large public issue they would work literally night and day until the business in question was completed.

Their secretaries and assistants would also work with them far into each night, taking down and typing out the various draft prospectuses until at last, after many hours of most exacting work, their material was ready for the printers.

The staff would then feel a tremendous surge of relief. At last they could have time off and return to their homes before midnight!

But somehow, this expected leisure never came. No sooner had one issue been launched, than Dunn and F. S. Pearson made haste to provide further issues while the public was in the mood to subscribe for them.

During those pre-war years, James was making and spending very large sums of money. He lived on a splendid scale, rarely equalled in that era and seldom surpassed even in America.

As the years of effort yielded up their riches for him, he was more than compensated for his poor childhood and the privations he had endured as a boy.

Sir Douglas Hazen, then Premier of the Province of New Brunswick, wrote from London to W. H. Thorne in Saint John, New Brunswick, on June 13, 1911:

"A New Brunswicker who has made a tremendous success here is a young man of Bathurst, 'Jimmy Dunn'. We were at the International Horse Show at Olympia yesterday with him. He has 12 horses entered in the competition, and from what I can learn is regarded as a very substantial man here and is worth a great deal of money.

"He is a remarkably good style of fellow and has founded a hospital at Bathurst, his old home. Like all men here who make money he goes in for pictures and has recently purchased Holbein's

'Catherine Howard' for which he paid the sum of £30,000. He has a country place about three quarters' of an hour's run from Trafalgar Square."

Fifteen days later, Hazen wrote to John Morrissy, the Minister of Public Works in New Brunswick:

"There is a young man here from Bathurst, Jimmy Dunn, who has made a success in the financial world over here and made a lot of money. He is a very presentable fellow, and has not forgotten he came from our little Province.

"My wife and I dined at his house last week, and amongst the guests were the Earl of Aberdeen, and Lord Pirrie, head of Harland and Wolff, and other prominent people. Our New Brunswick boys seem to hold their own wherever they go."

As a symbol of his success and energy, James Dunn liked fast, luxurious cars. In his early days in the City, he used to drive up every morning from his home in Coombe Hill, Surrey, in a magnificent Rolls Royce.

Mr. F. T. Sims, his personal secretary for many years, wrote:

"People would stop and stare in admiration at this superb vehicle as it stood shining opulently outside his office. At the end of every day's work, Sir James would stride to the car, his steel-blue eyes glinting, his chin out-thrust, while the chauffeur held open the door for him."

Sims recalls how Dunn once engaged a new

chauffeur—not an exceptional occurrence by any
means. On his first trial behind the wheel, this
man drove Dunn up to his office by way of the
Embankment.

The chauffeur was not yet in uniform and was
wearing a bowler hat, which an unexpected gust
of wind blew off for some distance across the
road. He stopped and ran back to pick it up.

On arrival at the office, James Dunn called for
his secretary.

"Pay him off, Sims," he said sharply, "and
tell him to take his bloody bowler with him!"

He was often impatient with members of his
staff. On a business trip to Berlin, Dunn was
booked with his valet, Harry Herbert Skinner,
in the same sleeper. The weather was freezing
and no heating was available.

James took to his bed and covering himself
with the only available blankets fell asleep. During the night he woke up almost rigid with cold.
He searched for his fur-lined coat, but could not
find it. "Skinner!" he shouted. There was no
reply. In anger he deserted his cold bed, and,
covering himself with a blanket like an Indian
shawl, he searched for his valet.

Where could he find the servant? It would
not be expedient to dive into each separate
berth. But James always conformed to the title
of the popular song of that day: "I want what
I want when I want it." And he wanted his fur
coat. Since Skinner could not be found he would
search out his secretary, Sims, who was making

the journey in a first class car without the benefit
of a sleeping berth. Sims, he believed, would set
things right.

Through the corridor went James and on to
the next car still in the garb of the North American Indian Chief. Passengers were interested
and intrigued by the strange figure. But they
little knew there was more to come.

Sims was there and, slumped in the seat at
his side, was the valet Skinner, sleeping com-
fortably in James's fur coat with a blanket covering his feet.

"Skinner," James cried. "Stand up, stand up,
to meet your fate."

The coat was stripped from his back while
the culprit explained: "I was only wearing it
to keep it warm for you."

James was not mollified. He scorned Skinner's
help while putting on the coat over a blanket
serving as a shawl.

With every evidence of extreme indignation
he strode off to his own place.

James, by this time suffering from semi-
exposure, reached into the secret pocket of his fur
coat where he kept a flask of brandy for just
such exigencies. There was no flask. James instantly turned in fury and raced back to Skinner.

Just too late! He saw Skinner drinking deeply
from the emergency flask.

"Get off at the next stop," James shouted.
"Walk home and when you reach London jump
in the river."

When morning dawned, Skinner appeared before James with a cup of hot coffee and a contrite expression. He was received in silence. A good sign, he thought.*

Such was Dunn's warm-hearted personality and his prodigal and impetuous generosity to those he employed that they appeared to relish his outbursts and certainly thought none the worse of him for them.

There was an incident when James was crossing Canada by train. He was travelling with Ward Wright, a Toronto solicitor, and George MacLeod.

James was observing some new diet. Periodically, he fell under the influence of some practitioner or dietician who would persuade him that he was eating the wrong food. At one time, he would eat nothing but vegetables, and then he would exclaim that such fare was only fit for the beasts of the field.

He would switch to platefuls of beef, or the yolks of eggs, even a diet consisting entirely of English farmhouse cheeses, which were sent to him from every shire—until he tired of them.

On this particular occasion, James was eating huge watermelons.

The faithful Skinner was in the kitchen of the restaurant car, supervising the preparation of this strange dish. He brought in half a melon

---

* *Author's note:* The account of events is derived from records made available to me.

and placed it before his master, who suddenly
changed his mind about the diet and told Skinner,
in very plain language, to remove the melon
forthwith.

Ward Wright took James to task for speaking
to Skinner in such terms in front of comparative
strangers. James replied:

"Ward, don't pay any attention to that. It
doesn't bother Skinner. You know, he loves me.
If he didn't, he'd have murdered me long ago."

The business career of this irascible and im-
pulsive man, although brilliantly successful on
balance, had also its disappointments. On one
occasion, Dunn was approached by the Hungarian Government with a view to floating a Hungarian Loan on the London Market. During his
early negotiations, he learned that F. A. Szarvasy, a Middle-European financier doing business in London, was also bidding for this loan.

James spoke to Szarvasy and suggested that
instead of being in competition with each other
they should join forces. This was agreed and
James Dunn and his new associate then enter-
tained the representatives of the Hungarian
Government to a splendid dinner.

Dunn was attended by one of his senior clerks,
which was in accordance with his usual practice.

Towards the end of the magnificent meal, as
they all sat back enjoying brandy and cigars
under the ornate candelabra, Szarvasy suddenly
started to speak very quickly in Magyar to the
Hungarian delegation.

Dunn had no idea what he was saying, but when the party broke up, Dunn said to his clerk: "It's in the bag," meaning, of course, that the Hungarian Government Bond issue would go through easily.

The clerk disagreed and asked Dunn whether his new colleague in the deal, Szarvasy, was a good and trusted friend. James replied bluntly by asking him to explain his doubts immediately.

"You may not know that I understand Magyar," the clerk explained. "Szarvasy was speaking to your guests at the end of the dinner, telling them to eliminate James Dunn. Instead, he said that he would float the entire loan for them on better terms."

The relationship between James Dunn and Szarvasy came to an abrupt end the following morning; ever afterwards he refused to have anything to do with business with which the Hungarian financier was even remotely connected.

Chapter 4

BETRAYAL AND DISASTER

*Courage is not virtue, but the necessary
foundation of all virtues. Virtues are the
ornaments of character, but without
courage there can be no character at all
and therefore no virtue.*

—C. S. Lewis

I find it fascinating to see how, side by side
with the career James Dunn was so successfully
carving out for himself in finance, he was being
prepared and equipped for his real destiny—the
building of the Algoma Steel Company.

At the time of the Hungarian loan he had no
desire or intention of involving himself in Algoma. And he had no experience whatever in
the management and direction of an industrial
empire.

In the year when James Dunn had first visited
London with the Professor of Memory and his
wife, an American lawyer from Maine, one Francis Hector Clergue, was also abroad. He had
been travelling in Canada as a tourist.

He visited the Sault Rapids, boiling out of
Lake Superior into Lake Huron, on the international frontier, with Ontario on the northern

bank and Michigan on the south. It was a magnificent, awe-inspiring spectacle. It stirred up in
Clergue a vision that never left him. The sight
of these thousands of horse-power forever rush-
ing to waste filled him with the determination to
harness them to turning wheels.

He returned to the United States, where he
formed a development company in Philadelphia.
With ample funds in hand, he built a power
house on St. Mary's river, near Sault Ste Marie.
Then he set up a pulp mill and a sawmill and,
finally, he launched the Algoma Central and
Hudson Bay Railway.

A chance prospector, panning for gold, found
iron instead. He was bitterly disappointed with
his discovery.

Not so Clergue. He was delighted with the
turn of fortune. He bought these mineral rights
and also the rights to four other separate deposits. He named the mines after his five sisters
—Helen, Elsie, Josephine, Eleanor, and Gertrude.

The ore was rich, abundant and easily extrac-
ted. Clergue, still relying on American money,
moved an entire steel mill from Ohio to Sault
Ste Marie to process it. This mill hammered out
the first steel rails to be manufactured in Canada.

Vast sums of American money—in all over
$120 millions—were poured into this enterprise
in the twelve years between 1895 and 1907.

The village of Sault Ste Marie became a lusty,
brawling city. Its future seemed tremendous, for

the potential wealth was illimitable. An era of enormous prosperity was foretold for all concerned in the Algoma venture.

The wheels would turn, the ore would be mined, the furnaces would blast, the railway trucks would carry the iron and steel across the country. Everything seemed to be set for a vast creation of wealth. But instead of coining money for the shareholders, the annual losses multiplied. Then came the testing time. Banks refused to advance further funds; loans were hurriedly called for repayment. Clergue and his mighty enterprises collapsed, like a barrage balloon shot down by an enemy raider over London in the Second World War.

Sault Ste Marie, once a city of busy streets thronged with shoppers and miners and their wives became virtually a deserted village. Families went elsewhere in search of stable employment. Of all those who had been associated with the dream that failed, Clergue remained the only one who still had faith in it.

When the American money wells dried up, Clergue, who was searching for support, heard of the fame of the rising young financier in London, James Dunn, and invited him to inspect the Algoma properties. Dunn accepted.

Together, the two men travelled the wild Algoma country, while Clergue tried to infect young Dunn with his own enthusiasm for his project. It was a difficult task. The evidence of the eyes argued against the promoter's eloquence.

Construction of the railway line had ceased; grass grew between the rusting tracks. The Helen mine had been closed down; only a few men remained to keep the pumps in operation.

But Clergue was outwardly undismayed. He waved one arm towards the blue and silent hills, and announced earnestly: "You will find a billion tons of ore in there."

A billion tons! It was visionary. It was incredible. The potentialities of such a discovery —if it really was a discovery—set Dunn's own poetic imagination aflame. As he said later: "I was just young enough to feel that he was right." In fact, Clergue was right.

Years afterwards, when Algoma was turning out 800,000 tons of steel ingots annually, as well as one million tons of pig iron and one million tons of coke, Dunn sent out geologists to calculate the extent of the ore still in the mines. They reported that it must be all of a billion tons.

But when Dunn and Clergue walked the Michipicoten Hills together, in the wild country north of Lake Superior, all this lay ahead; a goal so far distant it could not even be seen, but only imagined.

Dunn, impressed by the possibilities of the steel works with its own supplies of ore, began to buy the shares of this derelict concern, at nominal prices.

Could Dunn, the financier, find money in England to set the silent works in motion once more?

Clergue asked the question and anxiously awaited an answer. For his hopes and fears depended upon the word from Dunn.

Maybe there was a chance! Robert Fleming, head of an important London finance house with a widespread net of investment companies, might be induced to take the lead in reconstruction.

James Dunn and Francis Clergue crossed over to London together.

They were disappointed to hear that Mr. Fleming was shooting over his estate in Scotland. They applied for an interview and Fleming said he would see them at his home in the North.

On the off-chance that they might shoot with him, Dunn equipped himself with a special shooting suit of green tweed.

On the night of his impending departure for the North, James gave a party for some of his friends in the Savoy Hotel in London. It seemed that he had forgotten all about his meeting.

Then Clergue, carrying a small suitcase, with hat in hand and a mackintosh over his arm, appeared in the private dining room and stood silently in the doorway, looking reproachfully at Dunn.

Dunn yielded to Clergue's unspoken pressure and, without saying a word of farewell, rushed off to the waiting motor car. They just managed to catch the midnight train for Scotland, with Dunn's faithful valet, Skinner, scurrying in their wake.

On arrival at Fleming's house they were told

that he had gone off for the day on a shooting excursion. They were invited to await his return.

Clergue had not the temperament to go shooting and was left to wander about the garden while Dunn, who had not the temperament to wait for anyone, pursued Mr. Fleming to the butts.

He found the financier about to take aim. Such was Dunn's enthusiasm that he burst in on him even in this hallowed place and poured out an oration about the potential future of Algoma.

Fleming handed him his gun.

"Since you won't let *me* shoot," he said dryly, "have a crack at them yourself."

James seized the gun, aimed wildly in the air and fired.

Dead birds descended in a flutter of feathers. Fleming gave a shout of admiration at this feat of arms, entirely unexpected by either of them.

James brought down another and more important bird. He succeeded in persuading Fleming to buy from the Philadelphia backers, at a bargain price, a controlling block of securities in the bankrupt Algoma group.

Dunn and Fleming travelled to New York in the *Lusitania* on December 5, 1908.

As it chanced, my wife and I were making a return journey to Montreal on the same ship. During the afternoon and at dinner at night, James watched over Mr. Fleming. But in the long winter evenings, when Fleming went early to rest, James would join me. We talked mostly of the North Shore of New Brunswick, of the rivers, of Bartibog and Tracadie Gully.

After Fleming and Dunn had arrived in New York, letters were exchanged, and on December 19, 1908, Fleming wrote to him:

"The arrangement which I discussed with you for your own personal interest in the matter, in view of your having brought the matter to my attention, and to the attention of Dr. Pearson, and for all future trouble in the matter, was that you would be entitled to take one-fifth interest in the business which would be almost $200,000 of stock and $960,000 in notes.*

"Of course," Fleming added, "if an issue of new bonds is made in the future there may be an opportunity for you and myself taking an interest in the syndicate on the best terms."

Dunn replied on Christmas Day, accepting these terms and noting: "I will at all times be willing to give my efforts in the interests of the companies as you may direct."

Dunn's share of the transaction, though small, was significant to him for two reasons: he had established a connection with the great financial house of Fleming, and he believed that profits would be substantial. But it was as a financier that he approached the business. He had no thought of any managerial association with the Algoma Company.

James used to speak of the thrill that Fleming's

---

* Fleming bought the notes and shares at bankrupt prices. Dunn's investment would not amount to a large sum of money.

letter gave him: this was the beginning of the new Algoma, he declared.

He was wrong.

Algoma under the financial leadership of Mr. Fleming did not improve in money-earning power. Expansion was not the rule. Rather did contraction and restriction prevail.

The Algoma story was to be longer and more arduous than anything Dunn then imagined. And the end of the story was to be more glorious.

Meanwhile, Dunn, Fischer & Company showed no tendency to contract! Expansion was the order of the day so far as they were concerned. Their staff of many nationalities, drawn from various European capitals, was increasing almost every week. Indeed, it seemed for many years that almost everything James Dunn touched in the business world brought credit to him and profit, too.

By March, 1911, he and Pearson made a public issue of Rio de Janeiro Tramway Light and Power bonds.

In May, they put on the market the bonds of the San Antonio Land and Irrigation Company.

By November of that same year they issued the Mexican Light and Power Bonds.

Pearson was President of all these companies and Dunn was their promoting financier, possibly the most active in the London money market.

I went to London in the late summer of 1910, and although my friend James was exclusively

concerned with business and I was entirely occupied with politics, we met frequently.

My home was at Cherkley, Leatherhead, in
Surrey. There was a certain amount of companionship between my wife and Gertrude Dunn
at this time. There were frequent meetings, with
pleasant dinner parties and exchanges of visits
between Coombe Hill and Cherkley, houses
which lay within a few miles of each other.

Happy relations between James and me were
never disturbed. We dined often at the Savoy
and Brown's Hotel. Differences occasionally occurred at these social events, mostly political, for
James was a Liberal and I was a Tory. But our
disputes were always forgotten when morning
came.

Otto Kahn of New York, partner in Kuhn,
Loeb, a famous and important banking house,
visited me in 1912. He predicted that the firm
of Dunn, Fischer & Company would become the
leading banking house in the City of London.
Kahn said: "He is a brilliant financier."

I repeated these words to James Dunn and he
was greatly pleased over this recognition. It
seemed, indeed, that the future was secure as
well as brilliant.

And then, in 1913, at the peak of his triumphs,
James Dunn suffered a set-back of the utmost
severity.

His partner in London, Louis Fischer, defaulted and fled the country. He left behind him
not only enormous debts, but also incalculable

injury to James Dunn, whose credit in the City
of London was damaged and even destroyed.

Doubts were spread and serious accusations
were at first whispered and then spoken openly
in banking circles. It was said that Dunn himself
was the real defaulter and that Fischer was taking
the rap. There was, of course, no basis for these
rumours. In truth, throughout his career much
worse than the worst was spoken of Dunn. And
as I shall show by the written evidence of Fischer
himself the strictures directed against Dunn
were utterly false and without any foundation
whatsoever.

All Fischer's business affairs were left in a
complete muddle. The entire weight of his liabilities fell on the firm—which, in the event, meant
James.

The partnership committed him to payment of
the debts of his absconding colleague even to the
last farthing.

But how much money was involved? No man
could answer the question until the whole position was exposed to view. And that day might
be far off.

The future for Dunn seemed wrapped in impenetrable and dismal mystery. He might pay
and pay again to the very end of his capacity and
still find debts cropping up after all available
resources had been exhausted.

It was indeed a dreadful dilemma. But decision
could not be delayed. Dunn did not for a moment
hesitate. Fischer's debts must be instantly recog-

nized and liability accepted. The alternatives were to seek, if possible, a compromise with creditors, or to repudiate the debts and take the consequences of such a decision. He did not even consider taking either course. He asked only for time and patience. He succeeded in getting both from banks and brokers and even private traders.

I went to Dunn's house in Coombe Hill, Kingston, on a Saturday night in early winter. The lights were low and the weather cold and cheerless. As we sat together after a very good dinner, he told me the mournful tale of these financial troubles. He was like a man caught in a net. Every attempt to escape led to another entanglement.

If only he could get a final statement of Fischer's debts! If only he could fix a definitive sum as his maximum liability! But he was denied the solace of certainty. He had asked an intermediary to seek out Fischer on the continent and get from him a reliable account of the position. His efforts failed entirely. Then Fischer wrote him a letter, by hand, on a sheet of plain notepaper, undated and without any address.

"I am grieved beyond measure in having felt unable to accede to your request, in every way justified," he declared.

Dunn then sent out two private detectives in pursuit of the fugitive. They overtook Fischer in Europe but failed to make any impression on him.

Never in my long and intimate experience of men and matters, have I been confronted with a tale of such tangled strings. Never was my sympathy for my friend so vividly aroused.

It seemed as though one should say to James: "Well, you had better clear up the situation. Liquidate in the best way you can and start again."

I remember quoting to him the hackneyed lines:

> "Life is mostly froth and bubble,
> Two things stand like stone.
> Kindness in another's trouble,
> Courage in your own."

Yet it was made abundantly plain to me that Dunn's brave spirit was not in the least crushed or broken. He was determined to shoulder all the obligations, and he felt sure he could discharge them.

James Dunn's confidence, the indomitable manner in which he accepted these fearful and largely unknown liabilities, and his determination to pay them all in full, with no compromise whatever, and asking no sympathy from anyone, strengthened my admiration for him immeasurably.

One of his minor difficulties was in connection with Fischer's palatial mansion, Grove House, Roehampton, where many outstanding accounts were found.

But in addition to these debts, there were also small and yet involved duties, such as paying the sum of £500 to release Fischer from a contract made to erect a mausoleum to Fischer's own memory at South Norwood Cemetery!

James Dunn had tried to raise money by every possible means. And I was afterwards in a position to give some slight assistance through my position as Chairman of the Colonial Bank.

He put on the market his own collection of magnificent pictures. With bitter regret but without a moment of hesitation he saw these treasures stripped from his walls—the outcome of years of fastidious and loving selection—all vanished in the smoke of adversity.

By August in that year in which he had liquidated his precious possessions, pictures and personal property, the war broke out. James Dunn turned away from finance and gave himself over to other matters, as I will tell later.

He performed the sad and most sorrowful duty, as required by law, of informing the authorities that Paul Freytag, a member of his firm, was a German and that his uncle was Governor of Heligoland. Paul Freytag was interned.

Early in the second year of the war James was to sustain another sharp and painful shock. His agreeable association with F. S. Pearson, in a partnership of like minds, which had lasted through the years, came to a tragic end. Pearson and his wife were drowned when the *Lusitania* was torpedoed by the German enemy. Their bodies were recovered and identified by James. He brought the remains from Ireland and carried out cremation at Golders Green, according to the wishes of the family.

In his last years, Pearson had been plunging

into stock market operations in New York. It was an unequal contest. Dan Reid, a famous Stock Exchange gambler, and other experienced market manipulators were too clever for him.

Pearson's will made provision for the distribution of millions. But his estate was counted in thousands. His right hand had forgotten its cunning.

Pearson's death may have saved Dunn from future unsound adventures which he might have undertaken in loyalty to his old partner and which would certainly have ended in loss to himself and possibly in final disaster.

As for the Fischer affair, it had a strange sequel years later.

After the war, in the early nineteen-twenties, Dunn and his former partner, the German Paul Freytag, met again in America. They talked of old times and acquaintances, and Freytag mentioned casually that Fischer was also somewhere in New York. He had seen him but did not know his address. Hearing this, Dunn instituted a search for him.

Freytag finally learned that Fischer was living alone in a small hotel. He had been seriously ill. Freytag wrote to him, explaining that Dunn would be willing to see him.

On December 16, 1922, Fischer replied to Freytag.

"It is only today that your letter of the 3rd August has come into my hands," he wrote, "and although I had not intended to ever again communicate with you or Mr. Dunn, the spirit in which you write me after what I have done is such that I cannot refrain from writing in reply to express my deep appreciation of such unmerited friendship and undeserved kindness.

"You have apparently expected me to communicate with Mr. Dunn or with you immediately after the war. Only if I had been able to make a large fortune or to make good, would I have cared to be heard of again.

"As it is, since the evening when I left London, I have never failed to be conscious of what I have done, of my short-comings before, and my want of courage at, the crucial hour. I could not face Mr. Dunn again.

"If I had been in business alone I could have faced things and borne it alone, but such was the feeling that I had towards Mr. Dunn, a feeling of the greatest respect mingled with anguish . . . I could not face Mr. Dunn.

"No, after such parting, let it remain. What has happened cannot be undone. If Mr. Dunn has overcome the difficulties of that time and is today successful once more, I am gratified beyond words. Will you not then let me remain with my mortification in privacy?

"After the sad departure of Anna, my wife, in 1918, my medical adviser recommended that I immediately take up some steady occupation. I came to New York and took a position of active work, with directorship on the board.

"The deflationary period of 1920/1921 wiped

out the profits of the previous years and brought losses so that the parties interested, including myself, have about decided to discontinue operations. What I may do thereafter I have not decided. My health is improved again, and, from having been given up as nearly hopeless seven years ago, I have recovered well.

"There is in your letter one thing which of all others gives me the most intense pleasure and gratification, that Mr. Dunn has emerged successful . . . of all men I have met in my life, in character and ability, I esteem him highest."

Fischer was then asked to appear at James Dunn's hotel. It was ten years since he had run away from London in the winter night, leaving a tangled web of deceit and defalcation behind him.

Fischer was shown into James's room. There stood James Dunn, now a baronet, in good financial credit and held in high esteem, secure in his own career, successful in his chosen profession. Fischer, on the other hand, was poorly dressed, ill in appearance and under severe mental strain.

He was facing the man he had brought to the edge of ruin. The shadow of his dishonesty, his utter failure and his fear of impending tragedy, all marked him for their own.

Did Dunn turn away from Fischer? Did he say: "Evil has come to him who evil has done"?

Of course he said nothing of the kind. He extended to Fischer the generous hand of pity.

The man was in virtual destitution and obviously needed help desperately. The humanity of James Dunn prevailed. Fischer was given a job.

Within a short time, Fischer was working hard. And all resentment of the past and what had been—and what might have been—forgotten by Dunn.

Fischer died on December 18, 1935. To the astonishment of James Dunn, he left an estate of £41,000. His list of beneficiaries included Dunn himself, who inherited a Flemish tapestry which Fischer had purchased for £1,400.

James Dunn's humanity towards his fellows is nowhere shown to better advantage than in his attitude towards the man who had brought him to the door of the bankruptcy court.

"Forgiveness", wrote Epictetus, the Greek philosopher, "is better than revenge; for forgiveness is the sign of a gentle nature, but revenge the sign of a savage nature."

James Dunn too often appeared savage when some stupidity or folly or incompetence irritated him, but no man concealed a more gentle or kindlier nature under an armour of gruffness, and a harsh and dictatorial manner.

Chapter 5

WAR AND RECOVERY

An army is of little value in the field
unless there are wise counsels at home.
                              —Cicero

THE WAR WHICH came to Britain in 1914 led
immediately to a moratorium for all debtors,
covering financial commitments of every kind.
The ill wind which was to lay Europe waste
brought this good to James Dunn, that he was
protected in his over-extended commitments, a
consequence of the Fischer defalcations.*

The Prime Minister, Mr. Asquith, had confidence in the young Canadian financier, and, as
we shall see, events of immense importance
flowed from this relationship. The first sign of
that confidence was unusual. In the autumn of
1914, when the battle front was stabilized and
trench warfare had begun, James Dunn led a
party in his own motor, driven by his own
chauffeur, to report on military hospitals which
were being set up in large numbers behind the
lines. In addition to James Dunn himself, the

---

* During the War, James Dunn changed the spelling of Fischer
to Fisher. A gesture of recognition of the unpopularity of the Boches.

investigators were Miss Violet Asquith, Mr.
Herbert Asquith and Lady Cynthia Asquith.
Three members of the Asquith family—and
James! It was a strange mission, for which
neither Dunn nor his Asquith companions had
any qualifications.

His report throws an interesting light on conditions in a world which could hardly believe
that it was at war, and had no idea of what war
on a Continental scale would mean. Landing at
Boulogne, their car and baggage were passed
through customs without any examination, but
the guard demanded evidence that they belonged
to the Automobile Association. The A.A. sign
was on the front of the car.

Finding it difficult to get hotel accommodation
in Boulogne, they appealed to the British Consul,
who gave them an address of a hotel in St. Omer.
They drove there, only to find that the hotel had
been closed for twenty-five years. They tried to
send a telegram from the post office but were
refused because the message was in English.
When they turned it into French they were still
refused because they had no police visa for sending telegrams.

All these frustrations were dissolved by the
sudden and unexpected appearance of Maurice
Baring, uncle of Lord Castlerosse, who was serving in the Intelligence Corps. He had come to
Boulogne to buy lobsters. He had a magical
magenta-coloured pass that gave him the right
to send telegrams. It was also an open sesame

opening the door to living quarters and food for the party.

In their journey through France, Dunn and his companions met many men in uniform whom they had known in happier civilian days. Dunn's reaction to the war in its early stage was typical of the general reaction. He wrote: "On our way between Cassel and Bailleul a General Staff car (Field Marshal French) passed us going about sixty miles an hour and we got out of the way quickly." At Bailleul they saw their first German prisoners. They were big clean-looking fellows, some of them Uhlans, judging by their shoulder straps. "They looked very scornfully at us and as if they would take the first chance to escape.

"From all I can judge from the German wounded and prisoners I have seen they are a cruel, barbarous people. On the other hand, I feel I never till now realised what a fine race of men our fellows are; the Tommies always were men, never giving way to tempers in speaking of Germans who had treated them unfairly, nor complaining of anything."

This visit to the Army medical forces in France was a wartime curiosity. There were three members of the Prime Minister's family, knowing nothing of medicine or surgery, who cannot have made a deep impression on the Army medical corps. There was also James Dunn. It is not difficult to understand why he was there. He was preparing the way for greater things soon to come.

The Government was concerned at this time lest the Kristiansand Nickel Company of Norway should fall into German hands. They needed a man of determination, vision and personal courage to avert this danger. Dunn was recommended by the Prime Minister to take on the task.

He sailed for Norway, sighting a number of enemy ships on the way, and negotiated with Admiral Jacob Borreson, chairman of the Nickel Company. He secured an agreement that all the nickel already mined and being mined would be shipped forthwith to Canada for smelting and refining. The British Government agreed to pay the Norwegian company £100,000 a month in compensation for its immediate loss. But this was much more than a financial deal. It was a heavy blow to Germany, which had been able to buy all the nickel it wanted in Norway. Now Germany had to turn elsewhere, buying at a far greater cost and a bigger risk, for Britain controlled the high seas.

When warning was received through secret sources that Germany was contemplating the invasion of Norway, Dunn was sent back to put the mines out of action and to supervise the blowing up of the nickel on hand. The company was handsomely compensated by the British Government.

This was the first of his important war services. The second event took him back to the same coast. By January 5, 1917, Lloyd George was

Prime Minister and Leverton Harris, M.P., was Parliamentary Secretary to the Ministry of Blockade. He wrote to Dunn: "I may want somebody to go on a short journey to Norway, Sweden and Denmark on a confidential matter. Would you be open to go?

"If so, it would probably be necessary to start before the end of next week."

Direct transportation of food from Denmark to Britain had been disturbed by German action and there was a danger that it might be stopped altogether. Dunn had to negotiate an alternative route through Norwegian territorial waters.

The report he made on his return was a well-written and clearly reasoned document telling of his negotiations and of his journey to Bergen to organize the alternative route. His plans for increasing the supplies of food from the farms of Denmark were sound and worked admirably in practice. It was an excellent example of his energy and powers of improvisation.

Throughout the War, he did not neglect opportunities in finance. He made progress in clearing up the liabilities imposed on him by Fischer's defalcations. His credit in the City was restored.

The New Year's List of Honours in 1921 named James Dunn as a baronet. It was a proud moment, marking the end of an era of trouble, worry and disappointment following on the disappearance of his partner, Fischer.

The most remarkable of his associates at this time was Captain Alfred Loewenstein. He was

an attractive and volatile Jew whose Alsatian-
born father had been a banker in Brussels. He
was excitable and an exhibitionist who dealt in
words, not facts. His exhibitionism was apparent
even in his dress, which was usually flamboyant,
in contrast with that of Dunn, who always wore
dark suits. On the other hand, the flamboyant
Loewenstein neither smoked nor drank. Dunn
was not against every form of pleasurable though
innocent indulgence.

These two venturesome financiers shared one
passion or fad that brought them together. They
both fancied horses. Show jumping was their
speciality. Long after James retired from the
ring, Loewenstein built an enormous stable for
hunters and jumpers at Thorpe Satchville in
Leicestershire where the hunting community was
equally divided between those who loved him
and loathed him.

The business career of this Belgian was as
meteoric as Dunn's own, but whereas Dunn was
a visionary who created work for thousands,
Loewenstein was a pure financier, creating nothing except money for himself. When Dunn set
up his London firm in 1907, Loewenstein was in
charge of an important issuing house with considerable connections in Europe and America.
He was closely connected with Dunn from their
first meeting until he fell or jumped out of his
airplane in 1928, flying from Croydon to
Brussels.

Together, the two men launched "Sidro",

short for Société Internationale d'Energie Hydro-
Electrique, in Brussels, and also with the Dreyfus
brothers the British Celanese company. Dunn
and Loewenstein were the antitheses of each
other, but still they had certain similarities of
temperament. Dunn, who came from Irish-Scot-
tish Canadian stock, had been brought up frugally, and necessity had engrained in him the
habit of checking every enterprise carefully before he embarked on it.

Both men had the idea that "very important
persons" should have important entourages.
When Loewenstein went to America, he took
with him what was called "the Loewenstein
circus". Even his valet had a valet.

Going to the United States, he travelled with
four secretaries, two stenographers, a private
detective, a masseur and an air pilot. The bill
for their transportation alone was four thousand
pounds. But that was a mere trifle to Loewenstein. He boasted that in Biarritz he spent twenty
thousand pounds a week. He was equally lavish
in Barcelona where he rented every available
room in the Ritz hotel, had caviar flown in from
Russia and *petites poulardes* sent from Toulouse.
He had a staff of boxing, tennis and golf pro-
fessionals to keep him fit and to amuse his guests.
In his pursuit of physical fitness he was at one
with Dunn, but when it came to a business deal
the difference was clearly apparent. Loewenstein
would bombard Dunn with telegrams, letters
and messages by special messengers. They would

come from all over England and all over Europe as Loewenstein travelled from place to place in a fever of restlessness.

Dunn was deaf to Loewenstein's charges of procrastination. He waited till he was quite sure that the proposition was thoroughly examined before he would move.

They ran a kind of civil war between themselves by letter, telephone and telegram, but they remained close friends till Loewenstein died. That death is still a mystery. He set out from Croydon on American Independence Day, 1928, in his own Fokker plane, carrying with him a pilot and mechanic, a valet and two women secretaries. Loewenstein left his seat in the plane. It was claimed that he mistook the entrance door for the door of the lavatory. Subsequent experiments showed that it was not possible to push the entrance door against the rush of air except by an extraordinary effort of physical strength. The mistake, if it was a mistake, was not casual and absent-minded. The customary reason for suicide with big financiers was not present. Loewenstein left several millions, but the theory of suicide still persisted. What drove him to his death nobody will now ever know. There may have been a sudden and irresistible impulse to force open the door which was the door to death. Whatever the reason, Loewenstein disappeared over the sea and from James Dunn's life.

At this time I was deeply engaged in a campaign for Empire Free Trade, with tariffs against foreigners. Some tariffs would be maintained within our own boundaries, but unrestricted Free Trade throughout the Empire would be our ultimate goal. James Dunn was strongly in favour of our policy. He would not stand for Parliament, though I offered to work for his adoption in any constituency where a by-election might be expected. He did not want to be a politician and the prospect of office did not attract him at all. But he was generous in supporting our cause from his own pocket, and energetic in extracting support from other pockets.

James Dunn soon had other things to think about. The great American Depression of 1929 spread across the Atlantic. In this sudden and terrible hour of fear, his character stood out.

Many of his friends were going about, haggard-faced and utterly depressed because of the fall in the value of securities bought on borrowed money. But James Dunn, who had good reason to complain, never complained at all. He took his losses with tranquillity.

As the years went by and the Great Depression receded, Dunn became more and more involved in financial operations that ran into millions of pounds.

The purchase of one million shares of Boots Cash Chemists was an example of his activities.

The American tobacco firm of Liggett and Myers owned these shares, and a deal was negotiated to sell them to Philip Hill at £7 a share.

But the Bank of England objected to this transaction on account of the shortage of foreign exchange. Philip Hill therefore withdrew.

James Dunn held that the Bank had no power to impose its veto on a purchase of shares in a British Company from American holders. He then bought the shares at the reduced price of £6 5s. each, and sold them to the Tobacco Securities Trust of Great Britain.

This Trust employed John Todd to distribute the shares to the finance houses. Again the Bank objected and called on Todd, as the broker, to cancel the deals. The Bank still contended that the transfer of the purchase money to New York even for shares in a British Company would constitute a breach of exchange regulations.

John Todd was summoned to the Treasury, where the Permanent Secretary admonished him.

Todd replied that he had placed shares in a British Company on behalf of Tobacco Securities Trust, also a British company. Reginald McKenna, a former Chancellor of the Exchequer and Chairman of the Midland Bank, was the Chairman of Tobacco Securities. The Treasury should therefore apply to Mr. McKenna.

Todd thereupon left for his City office. As he drove along the Embankment, he passed Reginald McKenna, who was going to the Treasury. They waved to each other.

After seven o'clock that evening, McKenna sent for Todd, and explained that he had seen the Chancellor of the Exchequer. He had pointed out that there was no transgression of exchange regulations. The deal then went through in the normal way.

James had paid £6,250,000 for the Boots shares. A transaction of equal proportions at this time would amount to as much as £25,000,000.

He bought on a Friday and sold on the following Monday. His risk was big. So was his profit.

Chapter 6

HEART OF GRIEF

And David's Psalms had ne'er been sung,
If grief his heart had never wrung.
　　　　　　—Benjamin Schmolke

With some men, the personality is slowly eroded by the career. As wealth accumulates and responsibilities grow heavier, there is an impoverishment and hardening of the character. This was not the case with James Dunn, whose record has now been brought to the opening years of the Great Depression. The image of the man must not be lost in the narrative of his achievements.

In 1929 he had widespread interests. He had triumphantly overcome serious setbacks in business. He was busy and influential. It seemed that still greater financial power would surely come his way, although in fact his life was going to take an unexpected and fascinating turn. The financial tycoon was going to prove himself much more than a tycoon. Certainly there was nothing about James Dunn that in the least resembled the popular image of the financier.

He was not colourless, not cold, not completely absorbed in share fluctuations and market prices. Quite the opposite. The boy I had grown up with long before in New Brunswick had not shed his rich humanity. His business concerns were extensive and varied and he possessed more than his fair endowment of the fads, fancies and eccentricities that make the human race mysterious and sometimes diverting.

For while he was showing the most active participation in his own business enterprises, which had by this time assumed international proportions, James Dunn was not during those years a happy man.

For one thing, his marriage to Gertrude Price, which had seemed such a wonderful match when it had taken place, had not brought him the peace and content for which his restless spirit craved, and which, indeed, was essential for him.

Although his daughter Mona gave him pleasure and happiness, he was lonely and detached from his home life.

"There has been so little time for reflection," he wrote to me, "there is always something in each day to struggle for."

Certainly James Dunn's family must have found his restless, questing nature difficult to understand, and it must have been especially so to someone of the temperament of his wife Gertrude. None the less, despite their differences, Gertrude and James shared many dear and real friends. Intimate relations prevailed between Mrs. Asquith and the Dunns. A sincere friendship had developed. Gertrude asked Mrs. Asquith to present her daughter Mona and herself

at Court. Then it was that the former Prime
Minister's wife wrote to James complaining of
his senseless quarrels with Gertrude. Life in
London with the children would be the reasonable plan for her. James could go in and out as
he desired. A good secretary to run the house,
keep the accounts and manage the servants was
Mrs. Asquith's advice. If the recommendations
were accepted then she would make the presenta-
tions at Court.

I do not know what his reply was to this
strange message, but I do know he did his best
to live on agreeable terms with a person of completely opposite temperament. He was a man of
method and action himself, and could not easily
suffer others who lacked these qualities.

I also know that he accepted Margot Asquith's
advice in the spirit of friendliness in which she
intended it. Years later, when she wrote to him
that she was broke, she reminded him that he had
given her the only lovely fur coat she ever had.

When Mrs. Asquith had to sell her home,
where James had so often been a welcome guest,
he secretly sent his representatives to the sale
to buy much of the furniture for the highest
possible prices. But the marriage which Mrs.
Asquith had tried to save came to shipwreck.

After long consideration, Dunn felt that the
wisest course, in the interests of both Gertrude,
himself and their family, was for them to separate.

In December, 1924, he wrote a letter to his
wife:

"I am greatly distressed to have to write this letter, because I have still affection and respect for you. But I think you must have realised by this time that our temperaments are so much at variance and our views so divergent that our continuing together would bring no happiness to either of us."

It is a formal letter and somewhat harsh in its brevity and objectiveness. But no doubt the text was agreed, and for reasons which were to become apparent when James made a second marriage.

The marriage with Gertrude was dissolved in the following year, and James Dunn sought happiness with a young woman of rare beauty, with matchless colouring, possessed of wit and understanding. Her name? Irene Clarice, the ex-Marchioness of Queensberry.

I was their best man at the wedding in Paris. We sat in chairs while the ceremony was carried through in French by the local Mayor. Then we had a party afterwards, in the Ritz Hotel in the Place Vendôme. A number of his friends had come over from London. We all enjoyed ourselves.

James wrote to me on January 17, 1926: "I cannot tell you how much I appreciate your breaking your holiday at Nice to see me properly married and also, in appropriate language, to inform the world of the fact."

Anne, the only child of this marriage, was born in 1929. Dunn's friends hoped that this union would usher in a time of real and abiding happiness for him. He had so much to give to the world, but he needed desperately—far more than most men—to have the right background of tranquillity and companionship in which his genius could blossom to maturity.

For a time all was serene. Then there occurred a tragedy which dimmed the brightness of his new-found happiness and hopes. His beloved daughter Mona fell ill and died.

Mona Dunn was a most unusual girl, cast in her father's image and sharing his love of life and gaiety to a highly unusual degree. They had so much in common, not least an abiding love of horses; she had been a constant and successful rider at national horse shows since her ninth birthday.

My first memory of Mona is of a tiny girl in a perambulator in the street in Montreal struggling violently with her nurse, who was trying to apply disciplinary measures. Another family friend interfered, with the result that the nurse was reprimanded. I confess my sympathies were with the nurse.

The more vivid a personality, the harder it is to put down in words. How then describe Mona's genius? It took the form of an intense originality of view poured out in a rich flow of talk—coruscating, inexhaustible. Yet hers was a mind essentially sympathetic and receptive. In fact, I think it was her very plasticity which rendered her genius abortive. If Mona had been a boy it

MONA DUNN   Sir William Orpen

"I never loved a tree or flower,
But 'twas the first to fade away."

might have been different, for boys have a medium
of expression of some kind forced upon them by
life. Women must create their own medium.

On turning from the intellect to the character,
one saw the same qualities reproduced. Like all
people of genius she was a stormy little soul. But
she was so receptive of love that no one could
help loving her.

At the age of 23, on February 21, 1925, Mona
Dunn had married Edmund Tattersall of the 5th
Dragoon Guards. He had won a D.S.O. in the
First World War, and was a member of the
famous racing family. The wedding took place
in St. George's Church, Paris. Her father gave
her away. After a breakfast at the Ritz Hotel,
the young married couple left for Dunn's house
at Cap Ferrat, in the South of France. By 1927,
Mrs. Tattersall was staying with her father, who
had taken a lease of Sutton Place, now Paul
Getty's splendid palace near Guildford in Surrey.
Late in May, she gave birth to a baby daughter,
and I sent her a telegram: "Mona, my darling,
shall I love the new as much as I adore the old?"

On May 30 she wrote to me asking whether
I would be godfather to the child.

"I want to ask you to do something for me
but I shall not be in the least degree offended if
you find it difficult or tiresome," she wrote.
"You have always been one of my best friends
all my life, and I would rather you were godfather to my baby than anyone else in the world.

"Would you do this for me or is it too much

outside your line? In the one case I shall be
more pleased than I can tell you, and in the other
I shall perfectly understand."

My answer was: "I am delighted to be chosen,
and only wish you had twins, so that I might
be godfather twice over."

I had a further letter from her, towards the
end of that year, telling me that Monica, her
daughter, was to be christened at Christ Church,
Hertford Street. She relieved me from the necessity of attendance, for I was in great personal
trouble at that time. She explained that Lady
McGowan would be there as godmother. I told
Mona that I would also go. The christening duly
took place on January 22, 1928.

And within that year Mona was dead in Paris,
only a short distance from the church where she
had been married.

It happened with a suddenness that still chills
me, even after all these years.

In December, I travelled up to Lincolnshire
to visit two old friends of mine, Lord and Lady
Brownlow at their home, Belton House, near
Grantham, for I was also godfather to their
daughter, Caroline Elizabeth Maud. I was late
in returning to London on the following day.
There had been an explosion near the station,
and the roads were blocked. So I was delayed in
reaching Stornoway House, my London home.

When I finally arrived, I found an urgent message awaiting me from Gertrude Dunn. Would
I telephone her as soon as I returned?

"Max," she said, after I got through, "Mona is dying in Paris. She has only two hours to live."

James Dunn was in mid-Atlantic, returning from America with the second Lady Dunn. I sent him a telegram of warning and prepared to leave for Paris immediately. But before I could do so, news came that Mona had died.

I went to meet James on his return to try and console him, as he had so recently consoled me in trouble and bereavement.

We spent most of the night talking together. He was almost unable to believe the news.

There was little that I could tell him. She had gone to Paris on a Friday to visit friends. She told me she intended to stay until Christmas.

On the following Tuesday night she was suddenly taken ill and was rushed to a private nursing home at Auteuil. Peritonitis was diagnosed; an immediate operation was necessary.

Her mother and her husband had been informed in London on the night that she was taken ill, but they had not been told of the impending operation. Her mother had tried to charter an airplane to take her to Paris, but it was impossible. And she arrived too late to be of any help.

Mona Dunn was buried on Christmas Eve in Putney Vale Cemetery. There was a service in the little chapel on a very cold winter day. The church was crowded with her close friends, and all of us were plunged in gloom, grieving greatly at the death of this extraordinary girl. She had wit, she had intelligence, and she had political understanding.

Lord Birkenhead, on his way to Madeira, hearing of the tragedy, sent me for publication this moving poem:

M O N A

OBIIT DECEMBER XIX, MCMXXVIII
ANNO AETATIS SEPTIMO VICESIMO

R. I. P.

How young she lies, five lustres barely past,
   'The happy profligate of all she owned;
Who drew on life as on a stuff would last;
     Who laughed, while flinging on the stake, and losing,
       never moaned.

Eyes frosty blue; which still could warmly melt;
   Some Northern legacy of golden hair;
Inapt dissembler of the thing she felt,
   Of gay and reckless temper; yet in reticence how rare.

Loyal in friendship; prodigal in trust;
   Of valiant fibre; over quick to give,
She smiled and loved; and trod the road she must;
   And died as those shall die who dare too vividly to live.

During the days following the funeral, I saw much of James. He came to Cherkley, my home in Leatherhead, two days after Christmas, and stayed for a time. But he was a sad James Dunn.

It was difficult for outsiders to comprehend the size of the grief and distress he suffered. Only those who knew him intimately could begin to understand it.

On January 19, I was leaving for the sunshine, and on the morning of my departure received a letter of such gloom from my old friend that at Southampton I wrote him a note before I went aboard the liner.

"I know that you are suffering from a great blow but you must not let it affect your whole outlook on life," I wrote. "These moods come to one—especially in middle life. I could give you countless instances—including my own. But in the end a resolute endurance is best, for there is no other way in which to face life.

"I know how hard it is to accept this form of advice or consolation. Nevertheless, I give it to you as the best I can offer out of my own experience."

Thirty years later, when Mona's daughter, Monica, was herself married and mother of a daughter, I was passing the cemetery in Putney and I went to the grave of Mona Dunn.

It was on just such a raw bleak, wintry day that I had been there last, for her funeral. I felt I was stepping back across the years; but now her father James Dunn was dead, and her mother Gertrude also. Of that group of four I was the only one left.

Her gravestone bears the simple inscription:

"Mona, much beloved daughter of Sir James Dunn, Bart., and Gertrude, Lady Dunn, who died in Paris, 19th December, 1928, at the age of 26 years."

And there is the familiar verse from the hymn *Abide With Me:* "Hold Thou Thy Cross before my Closing Eyes."

I turned away in sadness and walked back slowly through the avenue of tombs, remembering the lovely gay girl I had known.

I looked up the files and read the words of the obituary notice I had written in the *Sunday Express*.

"She has not left a single enemy or critic behind her. And of how many people of genius can this be said?

"And she has a little girl.

"It is less than a year ago that I stood at the font with Lady McGowan, and we gave, on behalf of a tiny infant, those tremendous pledges to renounce the devil and all his works, the vain pomp and glory of the world, and the covetous desires of the flesh.

"So swiftly after the Service of Baptism comes the Order for the Burial of the Dead."

Looking back over the life of my friend James Dunn, marked like a mountain range by the peaks and valleys of triumphs and setbacks, I know that this was his saddest year.

He had wealth, he had power and he had many friends. He was held in equally high esteem in the Old World as in the New.

But he had lost the one person he loved above all others, and without her all his success seemed flat and empty, all his triumphs were tired and grey. For a time the sunshine went out of his life.

It was many months before James Dunn moved again in the society that surrounded him.

Chapter 7

ALGOMA

In my end is my beginning.
        —MARY, *Queen of Scots*

THE YEAR 1934 was, for James Dunn, the time
of decisive change in his life. The events of that
year altered the whole course of his destiny.
Instead of being remembered by a small number
of people as an eminently shrewd and successful
financier, his name would go down to glory as
one who had risked everything in the stern con-
flicts of industry and, in the end, emerged as the
single-handed creator of a vast industrial empire.
At the age of sixty, when many men begin to
think gratefully of retirement, James Dunn, to
whom retirement was a disagreeable word and
an unacceptable thought, launched boldly and
dramatically upon a new career.

From now onwards, the theme of his life was
to be the Algoma steel enterprise.

The project may have been subconsciously
with him for some time. For years he had been
buying shares in Algoma at varying prices, paying as little as a dollar a share and sometimes
more. Between 1916 and 1918 he had bought
Robert Fleming's personal holding at a modest

price. His total holdings of Algoma in 1934 were, perhaps, twenty per cent of the common shares. It was, however, twenty per cent of the share capital of an insolvent concern. Algoma was in bankruptcy. This was the financial aspect of an industrial set-back amounting to a calamity.

The plant was there at Sault Ste Marie. But the furnaces were cold. The steel works were silent. Further north, in the rugged barren country beyond the northern shore of Lake Superior, amidst the savage beauty of woods and rocky outcrops, were the five ore mines, each bearing the name of a girl. But the mines, too, were idle.

The promise of Algoma was still there as it had been since the days of that perceptive American traveller Clergue. But it was promise still in abeyance, promise only visible to the eye of the imagination and only to be translated into reality by vigorous and tenacious industrial statesmanship.

What had happened to Algoma during the years since James Dunn first took an interest in it ? What had gone wrong with the fire of mighty endeavour that Clergue had lit and Dunn had nurtured ?

There had been, no doubt, lack of leadership. But deeper than that lay the fact that the general economic development of Canada had still, in the twenties, not reached as far as Algoma in its spread westwards across the continent. Algoma had come too soon. Canada had still to reach it.

There was not yet, in the Dominion, an adequate market for its iron and steel. Nor was there the financial backing available to carry it through the long years of adversity.

So Algoma had languished. And then, on top of the inescapable handicaps which were imposed on it by the economic stage that Canada had reached, there occurred in 1929 the opening of the Great Depression. The economic catastrophe which swept R. B. Bennett from power was, for Algoma, a crushing blow and, it seemed, a final blow. It was a blow directed against a business already staggering and likely to fall. Algoma went bankrupt.

The crisis that faced James Dunn in 1934 can therefore be simply stated: he was one-fifth owner in the equity of Algoma—an obsolescent and bankrupt concern. His fortune was invested in the company. The struggle for reorganization was, for him, a momentous issue. The situation demanded immediate action.

His first approach was a purely financial one. He thought in terms of a reorganization. The business could not carry the burden of debts. It was necessary to curtail its liabilities in one direction and another, to cancel debentures and to reach a compromise with creditors. Fresh capital could then be found in the hope of resuming operation on a profitable basis.

To this delicate task of negotiation James Dunn now addressed himself. He had the support of Nivison and Co. of London, a firm of stock-

brokers who had an important holding in Algoma. All through the events that followed, Nivisons never faltered in their backing for Dunn.
Support he certainly needed. For, very soon, two
facts became clear. Dunn must assume the active
direction of Algoma. And he could win the right
to give that direction only after a struggle with
a formidable but friendly rival.

Practising law in Toronto was Ward Wright,
a man of ability who was looked on with respect
in financial circles. Wright became a contender
for the Algoma throne with the support of powerful Canadian and American interests. Above all,
he had the support of the Bank of Montreal, the
long-time banker of Algoma and an important
creditor of the company.

Wright and Dunn worked together amicably
on the problem of reconstruction. Neither concealed from the other his ambition to gain the
mastery of the concern, if he could do so.

The decision between them came about as a
matter of politics. The Premier of Ontario at
that time was Mitchell Hepburn. Hepburn came
out in favour of Dunn, his personal friend. Ward
Wright was unacceptable to the Premier. Hepburn's choice was of decisive importance, for the
Algoma plant was situated in Ontario; his support for Dunn was, in effect, an approval from
the Provincial Government extended to the
Algoma enterprise if it had Dunn's leadership.
Besides it was hoped Hepburn would give a
bounty on every ton of ore mined. This would

be a form of financial assistance—in effect a government subsidy.*

With Hepburn's decision, Ward Wright withdrew from the contest. He gave his allegiance to Dunn, retaining his position as solicitor to the reorganization.

So it came about that in December 1934, James Dunn, with Wright as his Attorney, incorporated in the Province of Ontario a new company named the Algoma Steel Corporation. The assets of the bankrupt Algoma venture were taken over in exchange for 126,725 shares preferred and common, of no par value, in the new company. Dunn's shareholding under the terms of reorganization was not more than one-fifth of the common issue, far short of control.

On the third day of May, 1935, at the first annual meeting of the Algoma Steel Corporation, held at Sault Ste Marie, James Dunn was appointed Chairman and President. He had become responsible for the direction and management of the Algoma venture. From now on, his future would depend on results. Success meant wealth and power. Failure spelled loss of prestige and certainly the loss of his personal fortune. Yet failure had been the dismal history of Algoma— failure twice over, or even three times in 30 years of miserable and wretched strife within and struggle for existence with loss of public confidence without.

---

* In 1939 Hepburn provided by statutory enactment a bounty of $1.04 for every ton of sinter produced by Algoma.

Even the Municipal Government of the City of Sault Ste Marie was in desperate straits. Mr. Lyons, the Mayor, wrote to James describing his difficulties:

"Our City has almost reached the limit of its financing. For some considerable time we have had about eight thousand people on relief. We have a large amount of unpaid taxes and the City now owns about three thousand parcels of property including many homes and several business places. With the earning power of our Citizens reduced as it is now, it is practically impossible to collect taxes and on the last pay day we were unable to meet our City pay roll. We have used our loan from the Bank of Commerce up to the limit."

It was a solemn moment. For good or ill, James had mounted the driver's seat and had set out on a perilous journey. There could be no turning back. He must persevere and prevail. Yet the man who had embarked on this mission knew nothing of industrial management and was ignorant of the ways of commerce. Finance was the only subject of which James Dunn had any experience. And he was in his 61st year.

An interesting and indeed a decisive event in the selection of officers for the Algoma Corporation on May 3, 1935 was the choice of Marcia Christoforides as Assistant Secretary at a salary of two hundred dollars a month.

This young woman was born in Sutton, Surrey, England, on July 27, 1910. She joined James

Dunn's staff as a junior employee in 1930. A grave, slim girl, she used none of the adornments of other women. Her dress was plain yet neat and always tidy. Her complexion was a healthy combination of attractive colours with a texture as though recently exposed to sun tan. A long neck, high cheek bones and hair of a slightly golden hue gave her an exotic appearance. Her movements were free and she walked with dignity.

Marcia Christoforides was destined to take a part in the fortunes of Algoma which was almost collaboration in management and control, as I shall tell in this narrative. So much can stem from happenings that seem to arise by chance.

When I recall the casual circumstances in which James Dunn engaged this competent young secretary, I quote what Chamfort, the French philosopher, once wrote on this subject:

"Providence has been called the baptismal name of Chance, but a devout person would say that Chance is a nickname of Providence."

It happened at the height of the Empire Crusade in Britain (the political campaign), when young people wore badges to show their enthusiasm for the cause. One of these was Miss Marcia Christoforides, at that time just nineteen years of age.

Being a young woman of forceful views, she wrote a long letter to S. W. Alexander, now proprietor of the City Press, then an editor on the staff of the *Sunday Express*. In this letter, she put forward some well reasoned suggestions for our campaign.

Alexander, though a prejudiced Free Trade Gladstonian Liberal, was interested in what she had to say. But he misread her signature, and in his reply addressed her as "Dear Mr. Christoforides". He asked for a meeting. She replied by return, pointing out that she was not "Mr." but "Miss". She would like to meet him, for she wanted a job.

It so happened that Dunn had asked Alexander to find another secretary for his staff. When Alexander met Miss Christoforides, he was impressed by her youthful appearance and zest, and while he had no job to offer her himself, he remembered the need of James and asked: "Have you heard of Sir James Dunn?"

Christofor, as she was afterwards known to James and his friends, asked innocently:

"Who is that? Is it Dunn, the hatter?"

The only Dunn she had heard of till then was the well-known firm that sold hats.

"No," replied Alexander, amused, "he's a mad hatter all right, but he is also a prominent and very important and able financier. I think he may have a job for you."

So Christofor went round to see James, who had an office near by in Crosby Square. She arrived, looking very smart and wearing her Empire Free Trade pin. She explained that, while she was not fully trained for secretarial duties, as she had never taken on any job before, she could write shorthand and she could type.

Dunn was also impressed by her direct approach and he made up his mind at once.

"You can have thirty shillings a week," he told her. "Come tomorrow."

In June of the year 1930 the young secretary took her place in Dunn's office in Crosby Square. In July of the same year she faced disaster.

On her 20th birthday, July 27th, a storm blew up out of Norwich House, the London home of James Dunn.

I quote Christofor's account of the tempest:

"I had to discover for myself who the important people were and how they rated with Sir James. My knowledge of filing and various other duties was very limited as I had no office experience. I had to muddle things out as I went along.

"One day Sir James had said he was leaving early for Cornwall. He had not left me any instructions. A telephone call came through to him and it happened to be Mr. Walter Wigham, a partner in the firm of Robert Fleming, then holding bonds in the old Algoma set-up, and an anxious seller. I said that Sir James had left for Cornwall and Mr. Wigham was angry. He replied that he was just leaving for Vichy and would not be put off. So I said, very well, he had better go to Vichy. He answered: 'I thought Sir James was anxious to hear from me.' Then he cut me off.

"The morning passed and Sir James telephoned at noon. He said: 'Are there any messages for me?' I said: 'No.' Then he said 'Are you sure?' So I said: 'No, nothing of importance.' 'Well, was there *anything* for me?' So I said 'Oh, just Mr. Walter Wigham telephoned.' Sir James lost his temper. He named me as the champion fool, stupid and silly. He made reference to my gender and remarked on my ignorance. He then took the unnecessary precaution of informing me that he had not left for Cornwall. He was waiting for the Wigham message before leaving for the west country.

"I replied: 'I know nothing of Mr. Wigham whatsoever; I had no idea of his importance.' Bang went Sir James's telephone.

"I had hardly composed myself after this violent episode when the manager came up the stairs. He said he was very sorry but I was too inexperienced. Sir James had sent him to release me and say I need not come on Monday. I would receive a month's salary in lieu of dismissal.

"Thereupon I lost my temper.

"I told the manager that I had no intention of accepting this dismissal, that I thought it was most unjust and that I would forthwith write to Sir James.

"So I spent that Saturday afternoon at the typewriter, pointing out to Sir James that when I came for the interview two months ago I had made it quite clear that I was inexperienced, and that this was my first job. He had confirmed his

BEAVERBROOK AND JAMES DUNN

*"We have been friends together
In sunshine and in shade."*

understanding by offering me 30/- a week as
salary while I gained experience from day to
day in the office. I pointed out that, so far, all I
had gathered was a knowledge of bad language
which I had not heard before and that I would
wait on him on Monday for an interview to
further explain my grievance and hope that he
would see my point of view.

"I sent this letter to Cornwall by special delivery and let it go at that.

"The Station Master at St. Mawes telephoned
Sir James at 6 o'clock on Sunday morning to say
that a special delivery letter had arrived and that
it was from London. Sir James, thinking this
must be from Mr. Walter Wigham, got into
his Rolls Royce and told the chauffeur to drive
swiftly to the station, 26 miles away. When he
got the letter he was absolutely astounded to
read the contents, which I had taken a great
deal of pains to make as frigid and as fair to myself as I possibly could. Sir James, bordering on
a state of apoplexy, according to the chauffeur,
returned to the car. The journey back again was
a record for speed. But by the time he got to his
home, he seemed to see the funny side of the
episode. He called up the office manager at his
house on Sunday afternoon and said that he had
received a letter from me claiming that I had
been unjustly dismissed. The dismissal was in
abeyance, and I was to have an interview on
Monday.

"Monday arrived and Sir James kept me waiting until the middle of the morning and then rang. I swept in rather haughtily, feeling I had a just grievance. Sir James asked me to state my case briefly, which I did. I said that I came to him perfectly honestly, without any knowledge or experience and had told him so. I had been trying, though confronted by many difficulties, to inform myself as to his important contacts. I had received no help from him. I appealed for justice.

"Sir James was evidently impressed. In a cool and deliberate manner, he decided I had a right to my complaint. But he told me how he had been seriously put out by the confusion over Mr. Wigham. I said I was sorry and then he said: 'Well, you just carry on.'

"And from that moment I carried on until he died. I was loaded with more and more responsibilities, never relieved of any duties but accumulating new tasks."

Before many weeks passed by, Dunn had come to rely upon his young secretary. He admired her integrity and her industry. She disregarded ordinary working hours and never neglected her job. By another year's end, she became his indispensable secretary, and then his inseparable companion.

Christofor's financial ability and her keen appreciation of values rivalled the shrewd judgment of James Dunn himself. She shared and encouraged Dunn's readiness to take enormous risks with calm confidence.

One such calculated risk of Christofor's led on

to fortune. Under the guidance of James Dunn, she had invested her entire resources in shares of De Beers and Crown Cork and Seal at a time when market prices in the Great Depression had reached the very depths.

Time passed and the shares recovered handsomely. Then one day Sir Hugo Cunliffe-Owen, Chairman of the British American Tobacco Company and an intimate business associate of James Dunn, told Christofor that his mare Maid of Essex would win a race and make a lot of money for followers. Christofor decided to gamble all her fortune on this prediction.

De Beers shares, bought for 32/6, were sold at over 300/-, a profit of nearly ten times the original investment. Crown Cork and Seal, purchased in New York at $23 for each share, were sold at fourfold.

Christofor has written her own account of this escapade:

"These shares had been given to me by Sir James as an investment. He was at this time in Canada. I must make the sale unbeknown to him because I all too well knew his detestation of gambling in all its forms and that he would never permit me to take such a risk. On the other hand I also knew that Sir Hugo would never give me this highly dangerous and secret advice unless he had every reason to be sure it was safeguarded except for an act of God! Besides there was more to it than just a friendly tip. He wanted to impress me with his genuine gratitude for the help I had been in certain complicated family relationships and he hoped I would continue to exert my efforts in keeping the situation tranquil and that is why he broke his iron rule and gave me, in strictest secrecy, this 'hot' information.

"I girded myself with the armour of conviction that the gods would decide my fate. I set myself a crazy test embracing my lucky number SEVEN. It came off easily. Without further hesitation I sold the stocks through a friendly stockbroker who promised 'not to tell' and I handed the entire proceeds of the sale to Sir Hugo.

"As I have intimated Sir Hugo never gave tips nor would he ever be drawn into giving advice as to how others should bet, which, upon reflection, strengthened my weakening knees as the time for the race came upon us!

"It was a glorious sunny day. I found myself at the Paddock rail mesmerizing Maid of Essex. I was like a somnambulist but I was not entranced by what I saw. I felt faint at the sight of the favourite, the Aga Khan's gigantic, powerful bay. It grew to quite a monstrous size as I gazed fascinated in a queer horrifying urge to see it drop dead. Maid of Essex, when mounted by Harry Wragg, appeared to bend under his weight and with his long legs dangling either side of her slender body it was a case of more man than mare!

"I crept to a vantage point on the sun-drenched stand. There was a strange noise in my ears as I watched those gay colours flash

by to the starting tape. My teeth were chattering
and I was deathly cold.

"I kept thinking of Sir James and the Sword
of Damocles and whether I was in fact within
a hair's strength of deciding on an everlasting
sleep or a quick rush over a cliff. I looked towards Sir Hugo. His face was inscrutable but he
slowly winked an eye. THEY WERE OFF!

"I fumbled with my field glasses, a heaving
kaleidoscope trembled in my shaking hand, coming ever nearer—green, green, GREEN! The
waves of fortune were in full spate. The torturing
fact was the Aga's silks were ALSO green! A bay
was leading—the whole field seemed to be bays,
including Maid of Essex.

"In moments like these I feel one is in suspen-
sion and unable to register a thought or action
but I doubt if I were even breathing. The madly
dashing stream of pounding hooves were abreast
of us with just a few yards beyond to the finish.
The enormous power of forward thrust in the
vast strides of the Aga's horse were ghastly to
behold and right beside this monster was the
gallant little maid struggling valiantly with all
her might and main. They flashed past as though
welded together. Harry Wragg appeared to lift
his mount by some superhuman feat of arms and
body. She shot past in one heroic spurt of speed.

"With knocking knees I sank down on to a
seat. I was panting for want of air. Slowly I was
taking it in. A babble of voices, screeching,
laughing or crying, it was an infernal noise

really BUT the most wonderful music to my ears. MAID OF ESSEX HAD WON!"

The starting price of Maid of Essex was 8 to 1.

Christofor ended the day with a large sum of money. It was her first day of racing, and her last.

Christofor's own dry comment on her "day at the races" deserves quotation. "The horse race was exciting and the win was gratifying. Yet I feel sure the result could have been predicted."

Anyway, she could never be persuaded to lay a bet on a horse again.

She invested her fortune in shares listed on the New York Exchange. It was an era of stock market activity with rising prices. Christofor was now a woman of fortune. Her holdings increased in value. A trifling sum in 1932 had become, to her, an important estate.

This was the woman who in May 1935, just five years after entering James Dunn's service, became assistant secretary of Algoma. She identified herself completely and utterly with James Dunn's administration of the company.

Every Algoma issue, great and small, was discussed in detail between Dunn and Christofor. Her duties involved supervision of the financial records, so that the Chairman was kept in close touch with the money position. Her advice on personnel was sought and usually accepted.

Dunn himself wrote of her:

"To Christofor, who helped me to carry Algoma through its darkest days. Her inspirations often decided my next move."

The association of the two was an example of powerful team work, and fruitful in a measure which was not foreseen even by the most optimistic well-wishers of James Dunn.

When Dunn took over the direction he believed that basically Algoma was sound, though the past belied his confidence. True the bankrupt concern had supplied coke to nickel companies and domestic fuel as far west as Winnipeg. It had provided rails for the Canadian Pacific Railway, and the Canadian National Railways. Further, it had been an important producer of alloy steels for the Canadian motor companies.

There had been much production, but no profits. Just losses. The past gave little encouragement to those who hoped for a better future.

But more important than all this, Algoma's vast iron ore field in northern Ontario, the potential value of which could only be guessed or imagined, must be developed. But what useful purpose could be served unless the ore body could be mined to advantage? To James Dunn this asset of indeterminate value was an essential key to his future operations but only if the ore could be profitably smelted. That was the heart of the matter. He realized the inestimable importance of controlling his own raw materials as well as the factories and rolling mills to fashion them.

Then again with all its possibilities, Algoma had lacked one indispensable element—leadership. James Dunn, in the last decade of the allotted span of life and quite inexperienced in industrial management, would provide the leadership.

Dunn's arrival at Algoma was an exciting event. The Vice-President, Mr. John A. McPhail, gave a dinner party to 260 office workers, superintendents and foremen so that they could meet their new Chairman. In a brief speech McPhail outlined Algoma's policy for the future.

"Heavy fixed charges, holding companies and the tangled financial situation which has burdened the company in the past have all been swept away in its reorganization," he said.

"The company is not supporting any holding companies. Its organization has been reduced to the simplest proportions. It is hardly possible to estimate what holding companies have cost the company in the past.

"Sir James Dunn is not operating by proxy. He didn't vote himself a salary of $50,000 a year, not even the dollar a year he spoke of—we even chiselled the dollar out of him! He has taken stock for his holdings and he won't get one dollar of revenue until the company is on its feet and can pay it."

One local newspaper, reporting this, added editorially: "Never have we been left with such a glowing hope that the Sault's troubles have finally found their solution, and the dawn of a better day is not far distant in this long expectant community.

"Sir James is a firm believer in getting up in the morning and getting to work while the day is young. Six o'clock is his rising hour and he's ready to pile into the job right away. The men who drift out to the steel plant early of a morning with their lunch pails under their arms can know they have a boss who's up as early as they are."

James Dunn was always an optimist but he outstripped himself in his hope and confidence in Algoma. On May 19, just two weeks after the first annual meeting of the reorganized company, he cabled to Sir Hugo Cunliffe-Owen, the distinguished financier with whom he had carried through many deals, including the buying of one million Boots' shares: "Outlook very favourable." On January 16 of the following year he wrote more fully to Sir Hugo, showing that earnings in May of $49,839 had been built up to $109,000 by September.

"I expect to do better this year [1936]," he added. "I believe that within five years I can bring the present $6,500,000 market valuation of Algoma back to the pre-depression market value of approximately $50,000,000".*

In January 1936, James wrote to a friend in London about his plans for the future:

"After careful study of the present property and the steel market in Canada by English and American steel experts, I have decided to install

---

* Five years later (1941) the market value of the common stock did not exceed two and a half million dollars. Fifty million dollars pre-depression market value was indeed an overestimate.

a modern hot and cold rolling plant for flat steels and tin plate, the first of its type in Canada," he reported. "We aim at supplying one half of these steels now imported.

"My advisors estimate our profit with the present plant and the new at $3,500,000 annually.*

"Six million dollars twenty-year Bond money on favourable terms is offered me—the outside figure of cost of the new plant."

Confident though Dunn appeared to his shareholders and investors, he was faced almost immediately with a very great crisis which threatened to overwhelm him and the reorganized Algoma concern.

---

* James Dunn's estimate of profit of $3½ million annually was not fulfilled by events. In the year ending April 1942 the net profit was $414,000.

Chapter 8

TROUBLE, TROUBLE EVERYWHERE

We must brave bad weather as well as bear it.

—Scott

JAMES DUNN HAD assumed responsibility for directing Algoma at a moment when it was possible to think hopefully of the future of the enterprise but when danger was by no means past. He had shown courage—foolhardy courage —in putting so much at risk. He had arrived in the nick of time—he had even arrived a little too soon. Canada was not quite ready for a steel concern at Algoma. Doubts about the business persisted and came suddenly to a head.

The Bank of Montreal, to which Algoma was heavily indebted, suddenly refused to extend credit. It asked for repayment of the outstanding loans. This repetition of the events which had destroyed Algoma under Clergue in 1907 gave Dunn every reason for acute alarm.

The crisis in his life was, it seemed, every bit as menacing as that which had occurred a quarter of a century earlier when Fischer had precipitately fled from London, and left him on the edge of ruin. Dunn faced the challenge from

137

the bank with the same quiet confidence and
strength that he had shown on that devastating
occasion.

Dunn was in Canada. Morris Wilson, President of the Royal Bank, Canada's largest banking
institution, was staying with me at Leatherhead
in England.

Dunn asked me to disclose his position to
Wilson. The company's balance sheets were
furnished, which Wilson studied with care. An
inquiry was launched and representatives of the
bank were sent to Sault Ste Marie.

A meeting of Dunn and Wilson was arranged
at New York and in July 1937 the Royal Bank
took over the Algoma account from the Bank of
Montreal. Another crisis had been surmounted.*

This was a bold decision by Morris Wilson.
The company was not making substantial profits
and the debts were large. The Royal Bank was
taking over from another institution a big debt
owed by a shaky concern. If it turned out that
Wilson had made a bad decision, much criticism
would have been directed against him. It would
be fair to say then, that the Royal Bank showed
a measure of faith and hope at least equal to
Dunn's own optimism.

Wilson, as I will show later, had an even

---

* The Bank account was changed in July 1937. The next balance
sheet discloses liabilities to the Royal Bank of $3,322,000. In addi-
tion, outstanding notes and accounts amounted to $500,000. Another
$500,000 was owing for duties on coal imports, royalties and taxes.
It would be an understatement to say that the company was not
in a strong position.

more important part to play in the moulding of Dunn's remarkable destiny. The two men soon became close friends, and indeed they had much in common, both in courage and energy.

Wilson had a ruddy complexion. He was a robust, alert figure with a most vigorous mind and a genial and lovable temperament.

He was also a banker of high ability. With his years as a bank clerk behind him in Nova Scotia, where he was born, he became President of the Royal Bank before he was 50.

Wilson's command of public confidence gave him a position of authority and power in Canada throughout the depression of the thirties, and the war of the forties.

When I became Minister of Aircraft Production under Churchill in 1940, I at once appointed Morris Wilson as representative of the Ministry in North America. Although his duties were heavy, and sometimes must have seemed almost overwhelming, he served willingly without salary.

It was Wilson who informed me by transatlantic telephone, only a few months after his appointment, of the successful negotiations resulting in the American Government's dramatic decision to provide 3,000 new warplanes for Britain every month.

Within half an hour of hearing this news I broadcast it over the B.B.C.—and what an immense and encouraging impression it made upon Britain!

In December, 1941, the month when America entered the war, Wilson was promoted Chairman of the British Mission in the United States. The nature of his job forced him to fly a great deal. On these journeys he would take a place in the cockpit watching the instruments and seeking advice on flying technique. He wished that he had been a pilot instead of a banker.

Fortunately, as a banker his faith in Algoma and in James Dunn never failed or faltered. And he lived to see the full justification of his confidence.

Dunn's genius was at its height in these early years. He borrowed from banks and brokers in London and Canada to make large purchases of shares in the Algoma Corporation which strengthened his hold and fortified his authority.

British and American shareholders, discouraged by much delay and many disappointments over thirty years of futility, parted with their holdings at almost nominal prices. And Dunn was the only substantial buyer in the market.

Even though a combination of shareholders at this time might have turned him out of office, he showed no disposition to make terms with his critics—and there were many.

His indifference to complaints of his expansionist programmes aroused opposition and hostility among some of the directors of the company.

My brother Allan Aitken, a director, was dissatisfied with Dunn's administration, which he declared was dictatorial and secretive. He refused to attack his friend in public. Instead, he resigned and resisted all attempts to persuade him to go back on that decision. Other directors and officers accused Dunn of keeping everything in his own hands and of refusing to disclose his intentions. But he would not be restrained.

He declared again and again that the key to real and lasting success depended upon his absolute authority. He insisted upon his right to develop a supply of raw materials irrespective of cost. He felt it was essential to have resources in iron ore and coal sufficient for his own purposes, with surplus stocks for sale to other less favoured steel concerns.

The wild, rugged country north of Sault Ste Marie had from the beginning fascinated him. He shared Clergue's belief in the wealth of natural deposits that it held. Next to the hills containing hematite deposits there was another hill, standing more than a thousand feet above the level of Lake Superior. Tests made in the years before the war proved to Dunn that this mountain, which lay within the Algoma concession, was almost entirely composed of a low-grade iron ore known as siderite. This was wealth—immense wealth—but there was a condition attached to it!

At first, indeed, the experts held that the discovery was of little account, for the ore was thought to be useless, without commercial value. No means of treating ore of this type had been discovered at that time, and the quality was too low to be used in blast furnaces in its natural state. But the limitations which baffled the experts did not discourage Dunn. On the contrary!

He was convinced that this ore must have some use; and he determined to discover a means of utilizing it to further the prosperity of Algoma.

All the technicians unanimously declared that he was mad. They thought he had surely enough to do, enlarging and modernizing his steel plant, and giving daily inspiration to everyone by his own vigour and example, without also striving to find a process to turn useless siderite into something of value.

Moreover, the country was held fiercely in the grip of economic depression, and his decision in the face of strong and expert opposition called for sound judgment, energy and faith, three qualities which my friend James Dunn possessed in strength and abundance as great as any other industrial leader I have known.

Nowhere else in the world was an ore of this type being turned to commercial use. Dunn was confident he would be the pioneer of a new development. The know-alls were certain that he would fail.

He remained unmoved. He faced disappointment after disappointment. The most eminent engineers and geologists in the land declared he was wasting his money.

As thousands and thousands of dollars melted away and failure followed failure, it certainly seemed that Dunn had tapped a mountain of folly.

Finally, in the early months of 1939, after years of experiment, a treatment that seemed hopeful was evolved.

Even then, his engineers could not tell him definitely whether it would be successful until many thousands of tons of siderite had been mined and subjected to the new process.

I recall the excitement with which James Dunn finally informed me that the operation was, in fact, completely successful.

Today, this mine—this huge mountain hollowed out by his ingenuity and refusal to be overborne by doubts and uncertainties—provides an important and essential output of iron ore.

Again, Dunn was not content with one source of ore, gigantic as this might be; he pushed out exploration parties to the East, to the West, to the North and South, with orders to dig and discover new ore.

He continued to receive a regular report on the operations of the Helen Mine.

His search for new deposits was carried out at a time when his requirements of ore for Algoma were fully satisfied. Indeed he had surplus processed low grade ore called sinter which he was willing to sell, but there were no buyers.

Conditions in the steel industry in Canada in 1939 were not good, and the sinter was an entirely new product. Many owners of blast furnaces were unwilling to use it. They were difficult to convince that it could possibly be as good as ore of higher initial quality.

Finally, one concern, the powerful M. A. Hanna Company of Cleveland in the United States, was persuaded to market the ore on a ten-year contract, based on the price of Mesabi ore, and the manganese contained in the sinter was not paid for at all.

Dunn agreed to these tough terms because he could get no better. He had to have some outlet for his product in order to sustain the continuing operation of the mines. He must sell his ore or shut down this particular mining operation.

Within a few months of signing this one-sided contract, the price of iron ore fell by fifty cents a ton. Then war came. The situation was completely and dramatically reversed.

Instead of being hard to sell, iron ore of any kind was in enormous demand. Moreover, the manganese content in the sinter was suddenly of growing value.

Despite this, prices were frozen under the Canadian Government War Measures Act. The Hanna agreement became a devastating burden as costs of operations rose continually in a most alarming way.

This was a situation which, very soon, would bring Algoma into serious financial difficulties. But the onset of war had, of course, consequences for Algoma far wider than the effect of the Hanna contract.

Chapter 9

WAR AND LOVE

Without thee I am all unblessed,
And wholly blessed in thee alone.
                    —BETHUNE

THE WAR STRUCK Algoma like a cyclone—a
beneficent cyclone. No longer was there any
difficulty about finding a market for steel. A
period of almost limitless expansion opened although it also brought a severe increase in the
strain that fell upon James Dunn.

In one respect, too, the war brought personal
troubles of a financial character.

As Algoma was heavily in debt to the bank
and in no position to pay dividends, Dunn was
relying for income at this time on realization of
possessions and on speculation on the London
market.

In 1940 when France was overwhelmed, Moss
Samuel Myers, a London stockbroker, called for
payment of loans he had made to Dunn. But
shares had fallen in value and Dunn could not
pay. He refused to sell any Algoma shares to
meet the call. And indeed a sale of shares in any
quantity was impossible at that time of War
panic.

Instead, he applied to Sir Hugo Cunliffe-Owen for an advance against Algoma securities. He was refused.

Meanwhile, Claud Serocold, another London broker, agreed to carry the loans due to his firm. This news was a great relief to Dunn, who had suffered a severe disappointment through the refusal of his old friend Cunliffe-Owen to make him a loan.

Dunn had persuaded his New York lawyer, Forsyth Wickes, to purchase large holdings of Algoma at trivial prices. Wickes, he hoped, would keep these holdings and support Dunn with his votes. Instead Wickes became anxious about the course of the war and began to sell in small lots. As Dunn's failure to get better financial results from his management of Algoma subjected him to increasing criticism by some shareholders and several officers of the company, he was convinced that safety for his administration depended for the future on the purchase by him of the Wickes shares. He believed that, if Wickes's shares fell into other hands, the threat to his leadership in Algoma would take on a formidable aspect. He might be driven out of the chairmanship.

He was persuaded, and with reason, almost from the outset of his tenure of office that a conspiracy existed to oust him. Fearful lest certain interests should purchase these Wickes shares, he turned in desperation to one after another of the money sources, and without success. Yet Wickes's shares must be purchased. Thus his embarrassment in the critical year 1940 was increased. His anxiety was acute and two-fold. He needed money to pay the loans in London and money to buy the Algoma shares which Wickes was putting on the market.

Christofor intervened. She sold all her American holdings, her jewellery and every other possession. With the proceeds, she bought from James 15,000 Algoma shares at just under six dollars each.* The immediate crisis was surmounted.

By mid-summer James's capital resources were exhausted and every available asset had been liquidated, save only his Algoma shares which must be retained.

At the height of this financial storm his critics, his enemies, and many in high places demanded his resignation and reconstruction of the Algoma management. Rumours were spread throughout Canada impugning his financial stability. The British Government had launched a huge claim against him for taxes and penalties. With such burdens and in face of such claims, many unjust and some exaggerated, he might have been tempted to lay down his load. No such thought was in his breast. Resolution and confidence, faith and vision possessed him.

---

* As shares in Algoma were selling at $3 or $4 each, Christofor paid a full price for a block of fifteen thousand. In 1949 a bonus of four shares for one brought her holdings up to 60,000. After James's death she sold her personal holdings for seven million two hundred thousand dollars.

Then it was that he pledged large blocks of Algoma holdings to Montreal and Toronto stockbrokers.

His plight was desperate. Could he hold on? Doubtful. But also doubtful if in depressed and disappearing financial markets he could sell his large holding of Algoma shares at a price sufficient to meet all his obligations. Hardly had he mustered just the essential support among his friendly stockbrokers in Montreal and Toronto, who advanced him sums of money on the security of Algoma stock, when another crisis exploded under him.

His bravery flamed like a forest fire in his own Province of New Brunswick. Facing many enemies poised for an attack, including some of his own colleagues, he was confronted on October 26, 1940, with the first but not the last threat by the Ministry of Munitions and Supply at Ottawa to enforce the War Measures Act against Algoma. There was no denying the war powers of the Government. Authority was vested in the Minister, C. D. Howe. Management could be changed, Chairmen and their Boards of Directors must stand down when required by Ministerial order. Yet another terror was added to a terrifying situation.

The most dastardly blow, however, was delivered against James by base and wicked foes. His loyalty and faith in ultimate British Empire victory were challenged in dispatches from New York, reporting inquiries said to be launched by the Canadian Government from Ottawa and directed to circles likely to do him the most injury. Churchill was informed that my intimate relations with Dunn might be an embarrassment to me. Replying to his inquiry, I wrote in mid-October:

"Sir James Dunn is my oldest friend. I cannot be expected to pass any opinion upon his attitude to the War.

"His only letter to me in many months—copy attached—shows no spirit of defeatism. It is, of course, unusual for Canadians to consult the British authorities in the U.S.A. about their own citizens who are suspected of defeatism."

Thereafter we heard no more of these absurd reports.

To the personal worries of James were added heavy new responsibilities at Algoma. Every request for more steel was interpreted as a command, and he drove no one harder than himself. But by the middle of 1941 this unending strain was beginning to tell even on his astonishing constitution.

In the early summer of that year he wrote to a friend: "I am going one of these days to my Camp for a rest.* My doctors say I am wound up too tight and ought to unwind in my native forest."

By mid-July 1941, the first surgical interference of a painful and disappointing nature is

---

* The Camp was near Bathurst, New Brunswick, and known as Dunn's Camp.

adequately and vividly described by James himself. He wrote from the University Club, Toronto:

"I am now well again but I had a stoppage of urine at the Soo* and a great difficulty in getting a catheter in to relieve the bladder. Many different types of catheter were tried. If I could have got a plane I would have come here, but as there was no plane to be had, the local doctor went on trying different types and at last one got through. This does not mean a prostate operation, it just means that certain foods seem to inflame my bladder and colon so that I close up. The channel will have to be enlarged one of these days and in the meantime I have to be careful."†

Suddenly James was taken ill, and for weeks he lay in the utmost danger.

This illness was the most important turning point. For it had far-reaching consequences on his personal life.

In writing of a friend so dear as James Dunn, the temptation is always to pass over details that show imperfections either in his character or in his outlook.

His business and its advancement—at this period of his life, the growth of Algoma—was all-important to him.

Indeed, looking back, it is not to be wondered that Irene Dunn and he did not find complete

---

* The Soo is an abbreviation of Sault Ste Marie.

† James avoided a prostate operation for two more years.

happiness, although their marriage lasted for fifteen years. The long separation, when James laboured at Algoma in Canada and Irene played her vigorous part in the war effort in England, was yet another reason for their drifting apart. The remarkable thing was that they remained together for so long, and always on terms of mutual respect and friendship.

But it was not to last. The end was brought about by the sudden illness I have mentioned. James Dunn was given no warning of the seizure which threatened him with death.

On Tuesday, July 29, 1941, he was staying at Mr. J. P. Bickell's house outside Toronto. The day was hot and airless, and James complained of a nose-bleed.

At breakfast he had drunk, according to Christofor, the Assistant Secretary of Algoma, too many cups of strong coffee. Holding his handkerchief to his nose to stem the bleeding, he slowly climbed the winding stairs to his room.

Christofor followed him to apply ice in the hope of stopping the flow. She found him lying across the bed holding his chest.

He complained of violent indigestion. His face was ashen grey and he was cold. He looked desperately ill.

She gave him a sip of brandy and sent his manservant Skinner to find the name of the best doctor in town. Skinner returned with the alarming news that many doctors appeared to be fishing. One old physician, Dr. William Goldie, was available. Christofor at once sent a car to Toronto to collect Dr. Goldie, and advised him of the symptoms.

While they waited, James Dunn's condition appeared to grow worse. Above the city, the dark clouds of an approaching thunderstorm were gathering. It was an anxious, gloomy morning.

The minutes ticked by, and finally Goldie arrived with a nurse and an electro-cardiograph appliance. The storm had broken, and by some electrical freak of lightning the machine would not work properly. Even without its help, however, there was no doubt that James was desperately ill.

Dr. Goldie was not a man who believed in breaking such news gently. He told his patient that he was in a most serious condition.

"Is it a coronary thrombosis?" asked Dunn weakly.

The old man nodded.

"Yes, it is."

The doctor added that Dunn must go into hospital immediately. James asked that he might be admitted under an assumed name. Even in this hour of agony he was determined that no word of his sickness should leak out, lest the control of the fortunes of his beloved Algoma might be affected. For complete mastery of the concern was still far outside his grasp. The decisive voting power which he needed had not yet been acquired. And, in the delicate situation, adverse news about his health might well have a disastrous effect. He might be removed from his leadership of the company. Even Nivisons, his loyal supporters, might desert him on account of his ill-health. His fears were acute and his physical condition suffered further complication on that score.

He was slightly relieved when the doctor agreed to register him under the name of Spenceley. He hoped to hide this alarming situation from friends and enemies alike.

By this time an ambulance had arrived. The doctor had brought some sedatives, and Christofor put hot water bottles all round the patient, for he was chattering with cold, although the day was unusually hot.

Christofor, who was determined to nurse him day and night, set up a couch in the hospital room. There she slept fitfully by night. There she watched by day.

Her first need was for the services of a heart specialist.

She was told that Dr. John Oille was the most famous. She called for him. He was away from home, fishing near Bathurst on the Nepisiquit River.

This news might have daunted a lesser spirit than Christofor, but it only drove her forward. She telephoned to Bathurst, directing Mr. Harper Kent there to find this doctor on the river, wherever he might be, and put him on a private plane for Toronto. Her final words were true to type: "Call me here with no excuses but results."

So the day died and all through that night Christofor stayed awake, watching the breathing of James Dunn under morphine.

At half past nine in the morning, Dr. Goldie arrived to examine him and considered that he had much improved, for the initial shock of the thrombosis had apparently worn off.

The next day passed and the second night. James's nervous condition gave rise to extreme anxiety. He dwelt upon the imperative necessity of concealing his condition from those who were criticizing his Algoma leadership. His fear of rivals who might seize control of the Algoma company distressed him. His dread of colleagues on the board and in managerial positions who criticized his administration, his anxiety over the hostility of the Government Steel Control, his doubt of Mr. Howe, the Minister of Munitions and Supply, had become an obsession. Hospital nurses were forbidden to enter the sick room. The doctor had sanctioned the administration of injections by Christofor. All others were excluded. These duties and attendance upon the needs of the importunate patient occupied the night and filled the day with tasks.

Finally at half past four in the afternoon of Thursday, two days after the heart attack, as Christofor recalls, "a very odd figure in green plus-fours appeared." This was Dr. Oille.

He examined Dunn and told Christofor that the next few days would be critical. He would give him special attention. The Hospital Direc-

tion had been insisting that the patient should
be committed to their care. Rightly, they held
that trained nurses should take full responsibility.
But Christofor, knowing Dunn's fears and needs,
would have none of it. She and she alone would
give the attention so urgently required. Dr.
Oille intervened and quietened the opposition.

By the Saturday of this eventful week, James
Dunn was in much better shape. But it was not
until 17 days later, on August 19, that he was
well enough to leave the hospital.

From then on, until the day of his death,
Christofor, in her watchful guardianship of James
Dunn, took his pulse and blood pressure every
day and kept a record of her findings for the
remaining years of his life.

That James and Christofor had been attracted
to each other for many years was abundantly
clear to all of us in their intimate circle. But
it was during this dramatic illness that their
relationship deepened into love.

When James recovered, he believed that, quite
apart from the doctors and the drugs, he owed
his life to one person—Christofor.

Like Ruth in the Bible story, she had stayed
with him, and no entreaty would make her leave,
or even take a rest, while he had need of her.

Now he knew above all argument that they
were essential to each other. Even with his possessions, his acclaim, and his ambition, life without Christofor would be but an empty desert to
be crossed alone without comfort or solace.

The moment of decision was upon him: his need of Christofor was too great. He could not let her go.

They set out in a private railway carriage for Dunn's Camp at Bathurst in New Brunswick. The journey was a relief to James after his long, tiresome and painful confinement in the Toronto hospital.

From that retreat in the deep forest, Christofor wrote to Lady Dunn (Irene) on November 19, 1941:

"I have given him everything I have to give, and during his last illness I thank God I was given enough strength to help James pull through.

"It may seem strange for me to say this but I know James would never have been with us today if I had not kept an eternal vigil over him until he was out of danger.

"No one will know what those endless days and nights did to me—the rise and fall of his breathing as he lay helpless under morphia—the only comfort I could give myself was to hold his hand, making myself believe that in this way he could draw on my strength in the struggle.

"The nightmare of those tragic times will be with me forever. It was wonderful to leave at last the dark portals of that hospital which seemed to engulf him and to bring him safely down to his native land.

"As we neared Bathurst at seven a.m. the countryside was bathed in sunshine, and as I watched James lying on the little bed I had fixed up for him in the observation car, it gave me great joy to see his eyes shining with new life. He blew kisses to old land-marks on either side as we sped on our way.

"The arrival at the Camp and his boyish delight were memories I shall never forget, and no matter what happens I will feel well rewarded if his health continues to be as good as it is now."

Christofor realized how imperative it was for James to have the rest and freedom from petty worries that his stricken frame demanded.

She also knew the peculiar stresses and strains that had developed in his marriage, and in writing to Lady Dunn (Irene), she added: "If it is God's will that you and James cannot get along, because each of you require too much help from the other and neither of you are able to give that help, then please do not endanger James's health by a difficult atmosphere or any temperamental strain, because any awkward situation will bring on trouble where he is concerned and there is nothing whatever you can do about it afterwards. He will try to do everything as usual and you may be misled by his apparent ability to do so, but I warn you to treat him with the utmost consideration at all times.

"He has been kept very quiet, and although he may think he is doing everything normally, I assure you I have kept a very strict watch on his rest periods and in no way has he been bothered by trivial annoyances.

"If, as I have reason to believe, you are going to try and make a new start it would hardly be a fair beginning for me to be around.

"My feelings count for nothing in comparison to James's peace of mind, and therefore I will remain at the Soo for about a month putting things in order, during which time you and James should know whether the life you and he make together is going to be a success.

"If you feel you can give him the care and comfort he so sorely needs, you will be able to give him happiness also.

"I pray with all my heart that James will keep well. It has been such a long hard struggle for the last three months, and he deserves all the best life has to give him now."

But Christofor did not go out of his life; her part in it was not yet played. Indeed, it had barely begun.

She and Lady Dunn met in Montreal at the Ritz-Carlton Hotel, and discussed the situation.

It was a meeting between two women over the future of a man for whom they both felt love and affection.

Such conversations are not for other ears and eyes, but only for those who have the courage to shape their own destinies, painful though the decisions may often be.

It was a time of consultation and crisis, but finally the problem was resolved. Irene was free to divorce James with his consent. She took immediate action. James forthwith made a proposal to his devoted Christofor.

They were married at the Presbyterian Manse at Hammersmith, Toronto, at noon on Sunday, June 7, 1942. The wedding feast was held at J. P. Bickell's house Arcadia. The guests were Mitchell Hepburn, Premier of Ontario, Maurice Duplessis, Premier of Quebec, and others. Bickell tried to induce the bride and groom to fly over Niagara Falls. But Christofor declared she had waited too long for her measure of happiness and she would take no risks.

Instead the party agreed to renew the celebrations on the following Sunday at the home and farm of Mr. Hepburn. There a dispute arose over milking cows. Mr. Duplessis issued a challenge. A milking contest was launched. And to the surprise of the two Premiers and Mr. Bickell, they were beaten by the boy from Bathurst. They did not know that James Dunn had milked Mr. Armstrong's cows at Youghall, not for fun but for food.

It is not given to any of us to know the journey our life will take—or how long it will be before we reach the end of our particular road. Christofor and James Dunn had, in fact, nearly fourteen years left to be together. These years were without any doubt the most wonderful, most fruitful and most rewarding of their lives. It was remarkable and inspiring to see them together; and even apart they wrote each other poems and letters every day. Their love burned like a constant, undying flame.

I have already paid tribute to Christofor's devotion for her husband. Now I give the impression of another close friend, Brendan Bracken, who died in the summer of 1958, beloved and lamented by those who knew him.

On December 27, 1955, he wrote to Christofor, thanking her for sending him a Christmas card.

Although none of us knew, James Dunn had barely four more days to live; the curtain was preparing to fall on a life both urgent and dramatic. The last act was nearly over.

Brendan was writing an ordinary, everyday letter, when suddenly he paid a spontaneous tribute to the work and love of Christofor.

"Bless you, Christofor," he wrote. "You have looked after Jimmy very well. His bright complexion reminds me of a naval captain who had no worries in any part of his life, save when he first began to navigate."

Chapter 10

THE MENACE AND MR. HOWE

*A man hath many enemies when his back
is to the wall.*

—CLARKE

WHILE MUCH HAPPINESS was James's portion in
that year of his marriage, 1942, he also sustained
many worries and severe disappointments.

The balance sheet of the Algoma company was
not a satisfactory document. He owed the Bank
over 3 million dollars. There were bond issues
outstanding amounting to more than 2 millions.
The Company's liabilities for new and deferred
plant made up another 3 millions. Accounts payable exceeded 2 millions. Thus there were total
liabilities of about 10 million dollars.

With less than half this sum in liquid assets
and with net profits, after tax, of $400,000, the
Company's position was too weak for comfort.

James had some way to go before he could
relieve himself of his subservience to his creditors.

I have already referred in a footnote to a
bounty set up by the Ontario Legislature of $1.04
on every ton of sinter produced by Algoma.
Hepburn, the Liberal Premier, retired in 1942.
Premier Conant, who succeeded him, cancelled

the bounty. James was urged to enforce his statutory right. His claim was doubtful. He did nothing.

It was a tough year for James and worse was yet to come. He was not a wealthy man. He had parted with all of his assets except his Algoma shares, less 15,000 sold to Christofor. There were no dividends and indeed the financial position of the Company did not permit any payments to shareholders.

James himself wrote:

"We are becoming a fine company but dividends which I am earning and can pay would be so eaten up by taxes that I hold off paying them. Salary is the same. If I take 50,000 instead of 25,000 the taxes take an [word indecipherable] share of the whole."

Although this letter might have given the impression that he was drawing $25,000 salary, yet he never took it.

In early 1943 his health was impaired. He had been procrastinating over the need for a surgical operation. He avoided decision during many months and even years. The crisis was thrust upon him by his declining condition.

It was his second serious illness within two years. Dunn entered the Toronto General Hospital as a patient. For nine weary and distressing days and nights he was relieved of an infection. Then followed more extensive surgical interference resulting in the removal of his prostate gland.

He was not permitted to forget that his management of Algoma was subject to bitter attack. For long he had sustained his position against his foes. Now if news of the nature of his complaint should reach his opponents his resistance might be overwhelmed.

Exhaustive arrangements to conceal his condition from the public and business associates, indeed even personal friends, were planned and executed by Christofor.

It was announced that he would undergo a tonsillectomy whereas in fact he was subjected to a prostatectomy. Thus it was hoped that the critics would get hold of the wrong end of the stick.

A prominent nose and throat surgeon was retained to visit the patient every day. A large bedspread was requisitioned to conceal from several official visitors the tubes in use for draining the wounds.

By arrangement with the doctors and surgeons engaged on the case, the hospital nurses, male and female, were carefully selected and their duties were restricted to necessary services. For the rest the patient was under the care of Christofor.

Even in pain and distress James spoke almost every day by telephone to prominent public men and to managers of his works. All these extraordinary precautions, amounting to a cloak and dagger proceeding, were of little avail. For the attack on James's control of Algoma was devel-

oping strength even while his ultimate recovery
was in some doubt. Would his heart withstand
the strain? Could he escape another coronary
thrombosis? Was he capable of sustaining total
anaesthesia twice over?

He remained in the hospital for nearly five
weeks, until March 29, 1943.

When he was released his restless anxiety did
not subside. He was feeling the effects of the
operation and recovery appeared to be far off.
From Toronto he moved to New York, and then
went down to Florida, where he only stayed one
day before he returned to New York again.

He was certainly not in a fit condition to take
two of the most serious hurdles in his career.
And yet that is what he suddenly had to do—or
else give up Algoma.

Responsible authorities in Ottawa took a grave
view of the future of the concern. Rumours of
the severe nature of the surgical interference
were spreading through industrial circles.

Charges of grievous errors of management of
Algoma were freely circulated. Demands for an
immediate change of control were put forward
even by members of his own organization. Was
he fit to remain at his post?

Their campaign grew swiftly. Before long,
they were making representations to the Canadian Government.

As a result, on April 12, 1943—less than a
fortnight after Dunn came out of hospital—the
Canadian Minister of Munitions and Supply,

C. D. Howe, telephoned to Morris Wilson, Chairman of the Royal Bank of Canada, in Montreal, complaining of Dunn's management of Algoma. He made it perfectly clear to Wilson that, if the situation at Algoma was as bad as his steel advisors claimed, then he must do his duty. The Canadian Government would take over Algoma, or Dunn must stand down from the Chairmanship and Presidency of the Company.

The threat was deadly, for, in the conditions of the war, the Government was invested with authority over all productive capacity throughout Canada. Its power was almost limitless. As in Great Britain, management was required to conform to Government directives. Personnel could be dismissed. Management could be changed.

There were many precedents, particularly in Great Britain where several aircraft works had been taken over on the order of the Minister.

If C. D. Howe were determined to depose Dunn, there was no recourse, except the forlorn hope of an appeal to the Prime Minister, who would certainly support his colleague.

So when Wilson informed Dunn of his telephone conversation with Howe, alarm and despondency prevailed. Dunn prepared his defence. It would be a major catastrophe, he believed, to hand over the management and direction of Algoma to any other person or group. He had guided its fortune out of wretchedness; he had no need for more money to consolidate his plans. All he required was time.

But what would Morris Wilson do ? Algoma
had borrowed very large sums of money from
the Royal Bank for development work. In the
face of the demand from the Minister of Munitions and Supply, Morris Wilson might decide
to bring Dunn's control to an end. He certainly
had the power to force Dunn out immediately
by insisting on repayment of outstanding loans.
It would have been impossible to have met such
a requirement.

Therefore Morris Wilson's authority was also
absolute, should he decide to use it.

Dunn, weak and depressed from his operation,
totally unequipped for the move to oust him and
desperately alarmed by it, realized that the bank
might well prefer to have the Government as
their debtor rather than a private company already heavily mortgaged. The bank would naturally feel more comfortable under Government
control and Government responsibility for repayment of loans. The gravity of the threat to
his position could hardly be exaggerated.

Dunn anxiously asked Morris Wilson for
advice. Wilson replied that Dunn should refuse
to "step down" and should await events. Dunn
was heartened by this advice. It conformed to
his own ideas about the best answer to the
problem.

So, helped by the faith and friendship of Morris
Wilson, he jumped the first and possibly the
most dangerous hurdle. He sat firmly in his seat.

The good news lulled him into a feeling of

relief. He was surprised and depressed therefore to hear only a few days later from Thomas F. Rahilly, a vice-president and general manager of Algoma, who was in Washington, that Howe had declared: "The Government will take over Algoma."

Dunn reported this information to Wilson, who told Howe of the Bank's support of Dunn and asked for the disclosure of the Government's intention.

Howe replied that in the circumstances he had no thought of taking over Algoma. Thus relief came to Dunn for the second time. Another hurdle was behind him. He recovered from his illness in a hopeful state of mind.*

However, the attempts to snatch Algoma from him were by no means at an end. Only a few weeks later, in May, 1943, Mr. Thayer Lindsley

---

* Mr. Howe gave a different account of these events. He recalled that he was informed by his Steel Controller that Sir James Dunn was dismissing Thomas F. Rahilly and that operations would be in jeopardy if this happened. Mr. Howe telephoned Mr. Morris Wilson asking him to look into the situation, saying that if Rahilly was being dismissed a suitable replacement should be made immediately available. Mr. Wilson later told him that Sir James had a competent successor to Mr. Rahilly—Mr. David Holbrook. On receiving this news, Mr. Howe stated, he ceased to worry about Algoma. Mr. Howe maintained that at no time did he threaten to take over Algoma. The Company was a vital part of Canada's war machine and his only concern was that there should be continuity of operational management. At this time Mr. Howe did not know Sir James well and he felt that he had reason for anxiety about the dismissal of Rahilly.

Author's note: Mr. Howe's account is not accurate. Mr. Rahilly resigned from Algoma in August 1943. He was succeeded by Mr. S. V. McLeod as General Manager. Mr. Louis Derrer signed as Acting General Manager after Mr. McLeod's resignation in 1944. It was not until May 1, 1944, that David Holbrook joined the Company—and then as Assistant General Manager. He became Vice-President in November, 1946, and in September, 1949, Executive Vice-President and a director.

of Toronto, head of the Ventures Corporation, which had widespread mining interests and ample cash resources, proposed to buy from James 50,000 shares of Algoma for $1,000,000, with the right to take another 50,000 at the same price. This offer was accompanied by a warning that he should "go while the going was good". *

In the harassing situation of Algoma, many would have been tempted by Lindsley's money, but not my friend James Dunn. He realized the underlying significance of the propositions. The loss of 100,000 shares would mean that all hope of one day gaining effective control would pass away. Dunn's consent to the transfer of the shares would mean that he had resigned his chance of achieving absolute authority. This he could not contemplate. He rejected the offer forthwith.

In late May, 1943, I was staying at the Waldorf Towers in New York. I arranged a meeting between Howe and Dunn. The discussions were not friendly but the atmosphere improved before we parted. On July 1, I wrote Howe. He replied on August 10 that the meeting in New York had been followed by satisfactory arrangements. "Your word in his behalf," he wrote, "helped him considerably."

In 1944, Dunn gained control of Algoma. His own shares, supported by 15,000 held by Christofor (Lady Dunn) and 26,750 held by Lord

---

* Lindsley's offer for the shares amounted to $20 each. The market price was about $10.

Glendyne (Nivison) gave him a majority. The distribution was forty per cent of the capital with James and ten per cent with Christofor and Lord Glendyne.*

Now another crisis was awaiting James although this one was of a different nature. Algoma was losing heavily over the contract he had made with the Hanna Company of Cleveland, U.S.A., to supply that company with sinter. For, as we have seen, Algoma had contracted to supply the sinter, with the immensely valuable manganese it contained, at prices fixed in 1939, and frozen by the Canadian Government War Measures Act.

The costs of mining and processing the output were rising with alarming speed.

Dunn was crippled by this contract. It was tearing the heart out of his business. The losses every day were formidable. But he was committed to continue deliveries and to endure this drain on his resources for years to come.

This disastrous ore contract which Dunn had been compelled to make in the desperate situations facing him in 1939 was even more serious than the earlier emergencies. It threatened to wreak vast damage on Dunn at the height of his career. And there seemed to be no way out. Nevertheless, he faced the challenge with the

---

* When bonus shares were issued in 1949, Christofor's holding amounted to 60,000 and that of Lord Glendyne's family to 107,000. Glendyne wrote to James: "I am confident that I can direct the proxies in your favour for these Shares, at any rate while I am alive, so that you can count on receiving them as and when you want them."

same courage and confidence that he had always shown.

It became clear that unless some kind of change could be made in this contract, Algoma would not be able to fulfil its obligations. Accordingly, discussions were opened with the Hanna Company. It appeared that no agreement for increased returns could be reached as long as Government controlled prices prevailed.

The contract between the two concerns was also complicated, because it involved Algoma buying ore from Hanna at a controlled price as well as selling Algoma sinter to Hanna. Algoma was a market for the American firm as well as a supplier.

At last, after many protracted, wearying and worrying attempts to reach a solution, James Dunn organized a meeting in Ottawa on July 20, 1944, with Mr. G. M. Humphrey,* the President of M. A. Hanna.

Both Algoma and Hanna were to bring their full complement of lawyers and technicians in a final attempt to reach agreement. It was to be a most important and serious occasion.

All these senior executives met together in the morning in the Chateau Laurier, but, to their surprise, neither James Dunn nor Mr. Humphrey appeared at the conference table.

Then about noon, James walked into the meeting and informed the lawyers and executives

---

* Secretary of the U.S. Treasury from 1953 to 1957.

assembled that he and Mr. Humphrey had met privately and had reached a satisfactory agreement.

He handed the surprised delegates the details —written on the back of an envelope.

The solution agreed between the two presidents of these companies was ingenious and also simple. Mr. Humphrey changed the classification of the ore from Mesabi to a more expensive type and agreed to pay for the manganese content. This arrangement did not violate the Government's freeze of prices. Algoma was rescued from the pit of depression—thanks to Dunn's clever and unorthodox approach to a problem that might otherwise have been insoluble.

From then on, until Dunn's death, Humphrey, always a business acquaintance, was also a warm personal friend.

I have told already of Dunn's courage. As a young lad he proved himself physically courageous; but he also possessed mental and moral courage of the very highest order. This kind of courage is, in my experience, much rarer, and consequently more valuable. It is sometimes displayed in business by men of exceptional calibre. It was displayed by James Dunn in the development of Algoma ore.

The open-pit ore of Algoma's Helen mine would be exhausted in a few years. Most of the ore at the Victoria Mine was of too poor a quality to sinter in its natural state.

Dunn therefore proposed to dig deep underground workings in the Helen mine in the hope of uncovering another seam. Engineering firms and several independent American mining experts whose opinion he sought, assured him that this could never be a business proposition.

They pointed out that on account of the low grade ore no other mines in the region were working underground. Expenses would be intolerably high and the return would be low.

It therefore seemed that the Helen mine would have to close down as soon as the ore on the surface was exhausted. The situation was further complicated by the fact that the surface ore would be almost exhausted before the underground workings of the Helen Mine could be developed.

The only means of providing new ore, the vital raw material of Algoma, was from the Victoria mine, but none of the usual methods in operation could give this poor ore any commercial value.

Then James experimented with a new method, called the Sink-Float process. By this system the ore is changed into a high density mixture of water and ferrosilicon. The good ore is heavy enough to sink in this mixture and is recovered. The waste rock floats and is discarded. This had been tried once or twice in America, but only on ore quite different from that at the Victoria. No mines were practising this method in Canada.

Further, no equipment was available for large-scale experiments. The necessary plant would be costly.

James hesitated before embarking on this expense with no certain result.

Time was running out. He asked George MacLeod, the Vice-President of Algoma Ore Properties, to come and see him at the Seigniory Club in Quebec.

MacLeod reported that he was reasonably sure that the Sink-Float system would work; but he could not be certain.

He felt, however, that the enormous amount of ore involved, and the fact that the future of the whole mining operation was virtually at stake, made it a risk worth taking.

But, of course, he personally had no money involved in the project; he was not being asked to lay out millions of his own dollars in support of his theory.

Finally, they went to bed, and James promised to give him an answer in the morning.

Writing years later, MacLeod said: "I had been in bed about half an hour when a knock came on my door and Sir James came in, in his dressing-gown and slippers. He sat on the edge of my bed.

"He said: 'George, you think this process will work, but as I understand it, you are not certain?' I said: 'That is the case.'

"He said: 'I will have my car at the door tomorrow morning at eight o'clock, and I want you to go back to the Soo and get started on this programme immediately.' "

The results were brilliantly successful: the

experiment was a complete answer to the problems.

Dunn, by his unconquerable will, had rescued the Victoria mine from disaster.

In the following year, James Dunn had to decide whether to develop the Helen mine underground.

Here, an outlay of several million dollars had to be made before a decision could be reached.

Dunn took the risk. And the venture prospered.

As MacLeod says now: "He (Dunn) was able to distinguish between the advice of prominent people as opposed to his own people, perhaps not so prominent, but who intimately knew the ore body with which they were dealing."

Indeed, so great was Dunn's confidence in these men of his choice that when it became necessary to pour out even more millions of dollars to develop new deep levels at three mines he did not hesitate.

If his own people, men he knew and trusted, believed that a development would succeed, he backed them against the opinion of eminent outside experts.

On May 15, 1956, Mr. George MacLeod spoke at the University of New Brunswick. He gave a résumé of these years that had altered the destiny of Algoma.

"Sir James came to Sault Ste Marie in 1907. He saw a small community largely dependent on a very unstable steel operation. He saw that on the great water highway between Lake Superior and Lake Huron was a natural location for assembling the raw materials for a steel plant.

"In the hills north of Sault Ste Marie he saw iron ore, the life-blood of a steel plant. He arranged new financing for this industry and saved it from complete collapse.

"He did not at that time, however, personally direct the destiny of the enterprise. The company struggled along for 25 years, to a great extent dependent on intermittent rail orders.

"During the depression of the early thirties he recognised that putting money into the treasury of a company was not enough. It needed direction, and that he was prepared to give.

"From then on until the day of his death, his time and energy were largely devoted to Algoma. The struggling steel plant became the second in size in Canada, and ranks with the most efficient in America. The City of Sault Ste Marie doubled its population."

Nobody can speak with greater authority than George MacLeod of the vision and energy which James Dunn expended to build the Algoma enterprise up into greatness. For many men it might have been the worthy monument of a lifetime of struggle. For James Dunn it was the labour of his sixties and seventies, the years that are often regarded as a period of decline but were, for him, years of culmination and triumph.

Had he not formed Algoma Steel, and guided its destinies, this once bankrupt venture would never have grown to be a bulwark of production for the western allies in the war, giving work directly to thousands of people, and indirectly to hundreds of thousands, and prosperity to a growing city.

It is impossible to over-estimate what Dunn was giving to his country for the years ahead when he built Algoma.

Chapter 11

"MAKE STEEL"

Better pointed bullets than pointed speeches.

—BISMARCK

AT THE OUTSET of the war Dunn was seized with doubts and hesitations. He believed that if he went to England he would be given the opportunity to play an important part in the war. But he realized what Algoma could mean in that war. There, in command of that vast concern, he reluctantly decided, was the right place for him.

By building up the output he would make the largest contribution to the war effort of Britain and Canada, now desperately needing steel for tanks and guns and ships.

This decision was entirely wise. Yet it was not easy to take, or, once taken, to maintain. His friends in Britain were involved in the conduct of the war. His intimate companions were undertaking civilian leadership. Dunn often fretted.

I wrote to him on November 8, 1939, in reply to an enquiry he had sent me, recommending him to stay in Canada:

177

"It appears to me that the Germans have nothing more to gain now in this war and I can't imagine what Britain stands to gain either, for that matter.

"This country has been vindicated in the eyes of the Americans, and also the many other nations that look to us to show the spirit of Drake and Raleigh, and of Wellington and of Nelson, and of any other heroes that you may recall to mind.

"There is, however, a victor whose triumph shines forth more clearly as the mists darken, and the storm grows in intensity—and that victorious factor is Russia."

So, for a time, Dunn appeared fairly content to work on, building up the strength and resources and importance of his company. And from his great mills, which were working day and night, the volume of steel bars and sheets and rods and rails began to increase and multiply mightily.

When British arms had suffered reverses on almost every front, when France had fallen and Britain stood entirely alone, Dunn's discontent at what he considered to be but a passive part in the war, asserted itself again. He yearned for action.

On July 22, 1940, he wrote to me: "I know that if the day dawns when Churchill thinks I can do a worthwhile job, I will hear from you."

After consultation with the Prime Minister, I answered: "You make steel—that is a worthwhile job for us."

By October he was again restless at being so far from the hub of events.

He wrote: "I have another strong wish, that before it is all over I may have the opportunity of giving a bigger service than making steel in Canada so far from the Battle Front."*

But it was not to be. His future was inextricably bound up with the destinies of his country and his company, and his own contribution to victory.

Every week, every month, every year, the production of his steel increased. At midnight or at four o'clock in the morning, his great Algoma works were as busy as they were at noon.

Every night and every day the ovens, furnaces and mills, which then sprawled over 186 acres, were an inferno of activity.

I saw James on my many fleeting journeys to the United States, where I was seeking raw materials and also many weapons. The progress he was making in production thrilled me. Here indeed, at Algoma, the sinews of battle were being forged and strengthened!

Everything was building up on the most mammoth scale. Prodigious output of coke was planned and in the making too—enough to smelt all the nickel produced in North America—as well as all the coke Algoma needed for its own purposes.

---

* See letter to Churchill, page 149, which I wrote in mid-October 1940, repelling a false charge of defeatism directed against James Dunn.

Millions of tons of iron ore were carried in, and millions of tons of steel came out. This large group of blast furnaces in Canada produced so much pig-iron that shipments were made to their competitors for production of steel; for Algoma could not use all of its own semi-manufactured materials.

The works, by mid-1941, produced special types and qualities of steel for armoured cars, for tanks, shells, ships and gun carriages. Day after day, a new tinplate mill poured out square miles of "tin"—leaf steel coated with tin—for the canning industry.

The red cataracts of molten iron poured from the blast furnaces. Their dry scorching breath of fury, spreading over a hundred yards, was itself like the breath and heat of battle. And James was the General, the workmen were his big battalions.

These steel workers wore no uniform; indeed they worked stripped to the waist, sweating day and night, even in mid-winter, as though they were on the equator. But without them the battalions in uniform would have fought to no effect.

It was indeed a mighty effort, as the earth gave up her riches, and the genius of my friend and the skill of his workers harnessed them to glory.

Chapter 12

GLORY, GLORY, HALLELUJAH

Success is the child of Audacity.
—DISRAELI

THE LAST DECADE of James Dunn's life was quite the happiest, and, despite his enormous responsibilities, possibly the most carefree of his long life. His talents blossomed in a remarkable way. He became a man at peace with himself, in spite of his occasional eruptions, able to put all his tremendous energies into his self-appointed mission to build up Algoma.

As his business prospered, his wealth increased and his importance was exalted, he showed a decided and, to me, most unfortunate change in his political outlook.

I was unhappy when he told me that he was convinced the hope of Empire Free Trade had vanished. He was loud and even violent in his denunciation of the post-war British Government and its liquidation of the Colonies and Dependencies. "Burma and Malaya are going," he would say. "India has gone. The Dominions have been abandoned. South Africa is claiming independence. Australia is within the American sphere of influence, and Canada economically tied to the United States. I am now a North American," he cried aggressively; he spoke in favour of North American unity, though still insisting that he loved the English way of life. And he claimed that he had never surrendered to the English.

He could see no need for a barrier between Canada and the United States. As nature had not placed any obstacle between them, then, he reasoned, neither should Man.

His changed views were no doubt influenced by the growing business relations between Algoma and U.S. industrial concerns. His contracts with the M. A. Hanna company for the supply of ore and with General Motors for the sale of his steel products brought him into close touch with American tycoons; Algoma owned coal mines in Virginia; he spent long spells in negotiating in New York; these factors helped to alter his political outlook.

Then membership of the Iron and Steel Institute of America pleased him. He was flattered by the attention of Ben Fairless, head of the United States Steel Corporation, who once pointed out that James Dunn was the only steel company president on the North American continent who enjoyed the status of a proprietor and was responsible for his actions to no one but himself. During these closing years he had no need to fear any attack or criticism of his management.

The government controls were abolished. Ministers had no right to interfere. He was once more the absolute master.

Algoma was flourishing beyond even his dreams. Day and night the furnaces roared. The production of steel ingots, pig iron and coke had increased. The output of steel rails dominated the Canadian market. Alloy steel of many varieties was available, possibly 150 kinds.

And yet possibly the most valuable assets of this vast industrial concern were far beyond Dunn's immediate sight—120 miles to the north.

The conviction grew upon him that the mighty Algoma steel plant was of less importance than the vast treasures of ore which he had exploited in the face of discouragement. The visionary could see a reality beyond his dreams. By the end of 1949, Canada was becoming alive to the meaning of the ore developments being carried out by the Algoma concern. In December of that year, the Canadian newspapers featured the vital significance of these discoveries.

James Dunn was now producing far more of the raw materials required by the steel industry than his own great manufacturing empire could make use of. He was in the position of being a supplier to other and rival steel firms. In addition to these huge ore mines, estimated to contain a billion tons of ore, there were his coal mines at Cannelton over the border to the south. There were also limestone quarries in Michigan. To the east of Algoma lay the Canadian Furnace Company at Port Colborne, Ontario.

Management of Algoma was stabilized. David Holbrook, who joined the concern in May 1944 as an assistant general manager, had steadily gained the confidence of his Chairman. Indeed he would shortly become Vice-President and a director with executive authority. He was a reliable and trustworthy colleague.

But, impregnable as James Dunn might be in his command of raw materials, producing plant and management, he was still vulnerable in one respect—transport. He was dependent on the freight carriers of the Great Lakes. He could be held up to ransom charges which might cripple his business as severely as the Hanna contract had done in the early years of the war. He was never happy about this exposed flank and his worst fears were realised when Mr. William Coverdale, Chairman of the Canada Steamship Lines, carrying freight and passengers through the Great Lakes, ordered his ships to refuse transport of Algoma ore. This was a menacing situation, with the possibility of a combined squeeze between the steamships and the railways.

His reaction was characteristic and combative. At once he began to buy stock in Canada Steamship Lines. When his purchases amounted to less than control though more than any other single interest in the line, he demanded that management should be transferred to his nominees. Opposition mobilized against him and the possibility of a contest for the domination of the Steamship Company loomed over the markets.

A fortunate coalition resulted in the acceptance of Dunn's authority. Canada Steamship Lines passed under the control of Algoma.

Dunn's popularity with those who opposed him did not increase when he got rid of a number of Canada Steamship directors. He was quite ruthless in imposing his own policies on the Steamship Company and in demanding submission to his decisions.

The displaced, the disgruntled and the disaffected called him a buccaneer.

The old management was dispensed with and Mr. Rodgie McLagan was appointed to the direction and control. With extraordinary speed the earnings increased and the efficient and capable conduct of this important freight line has been maintained to this day.

By adding Canada Steamship Lines to his possessions, Dunn acquired fifty Great Lakes freighters, seven passenger vessels and three tugs. Subsidiaries included elevators at Midland and Kingston in Ontario; shipyards at Kingston, Collingwood, Midland and Port Arthur in Ontario and at Lauzon in Quebec, and hotels at Murray Bay and Tadoussac, Quebec.

By this time, James Dunn was looked on as a hero at Sault Ste Marie. In formal recognition of his "tireless efforts in building up the steel mills and creating a livelihood for the great majority of people who live in the Soo", the Mayor of Sault Ste Marie presented Sir James and Lady Dunn with the Freedom of the City.

To mark the occasion the Mayor gave them both a golden key on which was carved the City's crest and its motto: "Industry, Integrity and Intelligence".

In a speech the Mayor said: "If the place where a man's interests lie, or where he expends energy, or which he is anxious to see advance, make that place his home, then you will find it difficult to renounce Sault Ste Marie as your home city.

"Since your coming here some forty years or more ago, you have proven yourself to be one to whom the words on the crest, 'Industry, Integrity and Intelligence', can rightfully be applied.

"This key unlocks to you the gratitude of the citizens of Sault Ste Marie, for what you have done to assure them a livelihood and a security in making this place one where they may invest their savings and raise and educate their children without fear or uncertainty."

James Dunn had been criticized so fiercely and attacked so frequently that this touching demonstration of respect and admiration brought a characteristic response from him. He issued an invitation to the whole population of Sault Ste Marie for an "at home" at the Algoma works.

More than 14,000 attended—over half the population of the town. They ate no fewer than 30,000 hot dogs and drank 40,000 bottles of beer and soft drinks.

But James Dunn was to do more for the Soo. Delays at the airport annoyed him, so he bought the town's transportation system and a fleet of taxis. Though many purchases of this kind seemed to be founded on pure caprice, his knowledge of values never deserted him.

In this case, he resold at a profit. As a successful gardener is said to have green fingers, it might be said that Dunn had greenback fingers.

His purchase of the Windsor Hotel at Sault Ste Marie reminded me of Arnold Bennett's hero who bought the Grand Babylon Hotel when refused a drink of beer in the principal dining room. The Windsor Hotel displeased James. He complained of the cooking, a common enough grievance, and of the colour of the plates, which is an unusual cause of dissatisfaction. He bought the whole property—just as it was. He engaged new cooks and ordered attractive china. On the top floor of the hotel he had a complete section of the wall knocked out and an enormous pane of glass fitted in place of the bricks and mortar. Standing at this window, he could gaze on the industrial empire he had created.

In buying this hotel, he broke a resolution of long standing. Many years before he had joined with Loewenstein in buying an interest in the Negresco Hotel in Nice. They lost money, and James swore that never again would he touch hotel or restaurant property. However, he had no reason to regret his reversal of policy. The Windsor Hotel paid.

The purchase of the transport system and of the hotel were not business ventures, just ex-

amples of idiosyncrasy. Algoma was the great
and expanding achievement of his latter years,
and Algoma by the fifties was making him an
extremely wealthy man.

Success was now his portion. He was in col-
loquial terms "on top of the world". But his
enemies still pursued him. Shareholders, who
were discontented with his dictatorial methods
of directing the Company's affairs, found fault.
There were also investors who were not satisfied
with his refusal to pay dividends and his determination to plough the profits back into still
further expansion.

From their own narrower point of view, the
shareholders had some reason for their discontent. This was proved in a striking and ironical
way.

On January 3, 1956, the first market day after
his death, buying of Algoma stock pushed the
price up by ten dollars above the quotation that
had prevailed in the last days of his life.

The buyers believed that his rigid policy of
ploughing back profits year after year, to the
greater glory of Algoma rather than to the immediate benefit of the shareholders, had died
with him.

Chapter 13

HONOURS AND FAIRING

All things are done magnificently by the rich.

—from the Latin

DURING THESE LATTER years, Dunn was a very heavy operator in the Stock Exchange, in Montreal and New York. Indeed, it was from the proceeds of these purchases and sales that he drew large sums of surplus cash. He was getting no dividends from Algoma. On the other hand, the capital value of the Steel Company grew enormously. It seemed, indeed, in this later part of his life, that every enterprise with which he was associated served to increase his fortune.

Naturally the bulk of his capital gains came from Algoma, but he also had large gains from other sources.

When Charles E. Wilson, the President of General Motors, became Secretary of Defence in President Eisenhower's Government in 1953, he was practically forced by Congress to sell his General Motors shares. He gave Dunn the opportunity of buying them at the rate of 500 a day, at the middle price.

James accepted this offer, and on a rising

market, he naturally made a great deal of money from the transaction.

After Wilson retired from the American Government, he returned to General Motors. He presided at the annual dinner at the Waldorf Hotel introducing the next year's models. These were on display and shining brightly under the glittering lighting system specially adapted for that very purpose.

James and Christofor, sitting side by side with Wilson, talked of the display. Christofor said: "If only your cars looked as bright and shiny as these on exhibition here, they'd sell like hot cakes!"

Now Arthur Godfrey, at that time America's most popular television and radio personality, whose face was probably the best known in the country, was sitting near by. Overhearing this remark, he turned to Lady Dunn and said, chidingly: "But, dear lady, we are not selling hot cakes. We're selling automobiles."

James heard this comment and took offence at it. He turned to Godfrey and demanded: "And who are you?"

Rather taken aback, Arthur Godfrey replied: "My name is Godfrey."

James retorted: *"And what do you do for a living?"*

Now that Dunn had gained control of Algoma, it was possible for him to sell some portion of his Algoma holdings without fear that his position in the steel company would be imperilled.

Christofor, Lady Dunn. 1942.

"A long neck, high cheek bones and hair of a slightly golden hue."

In London attending the Coronation. June 2, 1953. Hence the beautiful tiaras.

Left to right: Mrs. Howe, James Dunn, Rt. Hon. C. D. Howe and Lady Dunn.

Thus in 1950 he sold 225,000 of his own shares to two subsidiaries of Algoma, the Coal Company and the Ore Company. For that reason he, of course, retained the voting power. In addition, he disposed of 67,200 shares to Mr. George M. Humphrey of the M. A. Hanna Company in August of the same year. It is impossible to tell what the Hanna Company paid for the shares. But an average price of 25 dollars a share would not be on the high side. The profits of this holding must have been immense.

This transaction was the subject of an interesting letter from Dunn to Humphrey in which he advised the latter to keep the shares in the Bank of Montreal "who are in many respects still the leading bank of this country". It was a generous remark, considering the lack of faith which the bank had shown in Algoma a few years earlier.

Dunn went on to say that there had been many bank robberies in Canada and the courts had held that a bank had no responsibility beyond exercising due care and diligence in relation to strong boxes:

"On the other hand, if you borrow any money against collateral in the bank, the bank is responsible to the owner for the collateral. For these reasons I never leave any securities in the bank without borrowing something on them."

In making these sales of Algoma shares, Dunn had one purpose. He wished to increase the cash resources which he could devote to Stock Exchange operations. He believed that, with inflation, rising prices in "blue chip" securities could be expected. And it would be possible for him to make large profits on which no capital gains tax was payable in Canada.

In fact, thanks to his triumph at Algoma, James became something more than a tycoon—a tycoon of a highly individual kind. He began to talk like a leader of industrial Canada. He was conscious of his wealth and power. But men who had minds of their own and no excessive disposition to be meek excited his respect.

Once, at the Waldorf Towers, James was on the way to his suite to change for dinner when the lift stopped halfway between two floors. It was full of passengers, all plunged into darkness, facing a blank wall.

Repairs were executed as swiftly as possible and then the lift shot up to the next floor. Everyone streamed out of it, thankful that they had not been marooned for longer.

James was irritated and called Mr. Dell' Agnese, the manager of the Waldorf Towers, on the telephone. Dunn shouted: "You can speak nine languages. Here is what I think of your hotel in one language," he said. "And it's an expressive language."

James had complete command of that one language in its most vigorous manifestations.

There was a similar incident of the failure of a lift when Khrushchov was staying at the Towers

and on the way to his apartment accompanied by
the manager, Dell'Agnese. Their swift ascent
was abruptly jerked to a halt and lights went out.
Khrushchov, groping in the dark, jabbed at the
various indicator buttons. Dell'Agnese, in a quiet
but highly worried state, earnestly assured
Khrushchov in Russian that these trying acci-
dents were what hotels had to contend with,
especially when they had taken monumental precautions to avoid them. He pleaded for patience
as he knew everything possible would be done
to rectify the trouble immediately. The staff
would know that Mr. Khrushchov himself was
trapped.

Khrushchov remarked dryly that Dell'Agnese
need not distress himself. No one would be
insane enough to try any tricks. There were
Russian buttons to press that would not fail.

The lift was swiftly repaired and Khrushchov
got out on his floor, right into the arms of his
guards.

He clasped Dell'Agnese by both hands and
said: "Don't panic. Thank God *you* are safe.
Dosvidania."

Dunn, like Khrushchov, was a travelling man.
He journeyed abroad with pleasure. And with
equal joy he would swiftly resolve to return
home again.

In repose he would sit with folded arms. He
seldom attended church and he never gave his
views on religious subjects. It is impossible to
say with certainty what faith he held to, though

he always insisted that he was a Presbyterian. And he never denied the influence of his early instruction in the questions and answers of the Shorter Catechism.

He had no ear for music. His favourite hymn was "Oh God, our help in ages past," and when frustrated, he would often shout out the lines.

James always liked to exercise in a bath twice daily, at home or abroad. Splashing about he would always sing the same hymn:

"Jesus loves me this I know
For the Bible tells me so.
Little ones to Him belong,
They are weak and He is strong."

Christofor (Lady Dunn) and the household would stand to attention until the noise subsided. Then he would go to bed, and Christofor would read aloud to him for half an hour, usually from some biography. When he fell asleep, three short rings conveyed to all members of the household an "All quiet" order. When the interval was over, the "All Clear" was sounded.

Stupidity irritated James intensely; immediately, he became touchy, disagreeable and even unjust. Then, his intimates said that he was in his "egg-shell" mood.

With the rapid development of Algoma, James Dunn's sense of importance (like Stock Exchange prices) began to expand.

The fame of this great steel works was spreading abroad in Britain, U.S.A. and Germany. A new steel-master had arisen! Another producer in the age-long tradition had entered the markets!

James Dunn had succeeded far beyond the dreams of his youth, but he was not content. What Kingsley called "divine discontent" drove him on.

As one philosopher wrote: "There are two kinds of discontent in this world: the discontent that works, and the discontent that wrings its hands. The first gets what it wants, and the second loses what it had. There is no cure for the first but success; there is no cure at all for the second."

The feeling that drove James Dunn down the long rich avenues of achievement was of the first kind. Not even his gigantic successes could ever completely assuage it. As a result, the evening of his life was more remarkable in every way than anything he had accomplished in the bright noon of youth.

Dunn was remarkable for another reason: he lived over eighty years, but he never grew old, nor did his faculties diminish.

His endurance became a legend. He would discuss some business deal long after midnight—and go out walking next morning before his companions were awake. He exercised every day, and, although I often made fun of his strange diets, I must admit that they seemed to suit him; he said he kept the fine, trim figure of a young man all his days. But not with complete justification.

"When thou wast young," recorded St. John, "thou girdedst thyself, and walkedst whither thou wouldest: but when thou shalt be old, thou shalt stretch forth thy hands and another shall gird thee, and carry thee whither thou wouldest not."

Old age can so often be a time of misery, dogged by feebleness, by the necessity to lean on others, by sickness and a general decline of all the faculties. There was nothing of this in the years remaining to James Dunn, those twenty glorious years between his sixty-first birthday and his eighty-first, the time of his real fulfilment, for which all his life had been a preparation.

He would frequently declare his intention of living to be a hundred and ten. Indeed in his eightieth year, he embarked on a twenty-year policy of expansion for Algoma.

He would speak to me of the proverb, "The farmer must cultivate his field as though he would live for ever." No one lives for ever, and it is given to only a few to reap where they have sown, doing good to whole communities and to mankind. My friend James Dunn was one of this select band of adventurers whose names live on long after death has gathered its harvest.

Before that sad day came, there was already recognition of the service he had given.

When he possessed everything most men strive for all their days and never achieve—wealth, power and love—more and more honours were heaped upon him.

In 1949, on the recommendation of Premier Duplessis, he was gazetted a King's Counsel in the Province of Quebec. He was delighted with the honour. He wanted to be remembered as a lawyer as well as a man of business, though he was too much of a realist to forget that his fortune came from vision and diligence in commerce. Of Premier Duplessis he said: "I do not ask anything of him—I just like him and therefore I back him." It would be right to say that James did truly back Duplessis when election times came around. And not only Duplessis. Other party leaders were beholden to him.

Honorary degrees were conferred upon James by the University of New Brunswick, Dalhousie, Bishop's, St. Francis Xavier, Laval and Queen's University.

He was particularly munificent in his benefactions to Universities. He spread his gifts between eight Canadian universities. To three of them he gave a total of fifteen annual scholarships.

He provided a chair of geology at Mount Allison University and a chair of law at Dalhousie and of mining at Queen's University.

Mr. McLagan, President of the Canada Steamship Lines, wrote me after Dunn's death, and with his permission I quote from his letter:

"For a tough individual, he had a great feeling of kindness for those whose usefulness was over such as pensioners and would ask, How is he going to live on that?—and would insist on an adjustment."

James Dunn said in a speech that, in this world, one only keeps the things one gives away.

As long ago as 1911, he was giving money for a Manse at Bathurst, so that the Minister could have a new home.

In the following year, he gave a chime of many bells to Fredericton Cathedral.

A hospital in Bathurst was set up by him, almost in the days of his youth.

Forty years on, in 1951, he gave another hospital, the Lady Dunn Hospital, which serves 3,000 people in Michipicoten, near Sault Ste Marie.

He also sent £100,000 to the Westminster Abbey restoration fund.

To recite a longer list of gifts would just be repetition, and repetition dulls the mind.

Chapter 14

ECCENTRICITIES

Call him not old whose visionary brain
Holds o'er the past its undivided reign.
For him in vain the envious seasons roll
Who hears eternal summer in his soul.
—HOLMES

THERE WAS A gentle as well as a strenuous side
to James Dunn. Colleagues in business, rivals in
finance and the world at large saw the strenuous
James. Some of them believed that there was no
other side. They knew a severe man; subject to
brief but violent storms of temper; at times disagreeable and momentarily unjust. It was the
price paid for the exacting and penetrating mind
harnessed to a discontent which was not always
divine.

But the man was complex and not simple and
those who knew him best were aware of a sweet-
ness of character underlying the formidable
temperament and of a love of fine and even
splendid surroundings. He was a devotee of what
he called "gracious living". Whether he ever
achieved it is a matter of opinion. Some of his
friends, with their own ideas of comfort and
grace, had doubts. Some of his business associates

probably thought that life might be more gracious for them if Sir James Dunn, their taskmaster, would only control his temper a little more successfully. But, beyond doubt, "gracious living" was something he aspired after.

He had lived in two houses in Canada, many mansions in Britain, a villa in the South of France, rooms in a Toronto hotel, and a spacious suite on high in the Waldorf Towers, New York.

His house at St. Andrews, in New Brunswick, was his chief residence. It stood beside the Passamaquoddy Bay, which is an inlet of the Bay of Fundy. There James dwelt most of the time and from it he sallied out to do business in Toronto or New York or to watch over Algoma, seven hundred miles to the West. The house illustrated very well the nature and the limitations of James's quest for gracious living, as well as the quirks and twists of his character.

It was called Dayspring, and had been built by a Mormon industrialist called Smoot (of the same family as the American Senator), who sold it. The house is a spacious structure with four oil furnaces and six principal bedrooms and too many bathrooms. It was said that Smoot, who made his money out of sand and gravel, spent 250,000 dollars on this beautiful but extravagant house.

It was bought by Algoma for 45,000 dollars. James said he required a retreat in quietude where he could meditate upon his many problems, reaching practical and sound decisions. Dayspring fulfilled his needs.

At once Christofor moved in. It goes without saying that no effort was spared to provide James with a suitably gracious atmosphere for his meditations. She turned out nearly everything and refurbished the rooms with attractive furniture and materials. She added a cinema and a library.

The total outlay on these repairs, renewals and betterments may have amounted to as much as 250,000 dollars. All cheerfully paid by the Company. Possibly some of the staff at the Soo may have felt that the price for anchoring James 700 miles distant from the plant was not unreasonable. But of course he dragged that anchor. From Dayspring to the Soo was not a difficult jump. As the Company supplied him with two airplanes and crews, four motor cars and chauffeurs, transportation was no problem.*

The most curious addition was, however, the work of James Dunn. To protect himself from unwelcome callers and untimely interruptions he had a nine-foot fence built round the gardens. The gate had no bell and not even a handle. Whoever sought an audience had to telephone to the gatekeeper. If his request for entry was favourably received, the gatekeeper was, in effect, instructed to lower the drawbridge and pull up the portcullis. So James Dunn in his determination to secure privacy, rivalled Jack London, the American novelist. On Jack Lon-

---

* After James died, his wife, Lady Dunn, bought from Algoma the house Dayspring, with furnishings, the motor cars and equipment.

don's front gate there was a notice: "No admission except by back gate". On the back gate, a notice said simply: "No admission".

The nine-foot fence infuriated some of the neighbours but not the lady who occupied the house next door. She would have preferred a fence twice as high and soundproofed too.

Lads from the town took to throwing stones and empty bottles over the high wall.

During one night the boards were painted with two objectionable notices: "What's done is Dunn" and "Don't fence me in".

James notified the local authorities that if the abuse was repeated he would abandon his home, pack up his possessions and leave the town to live elsewhere.

Thereafter all was silence.

In contrast, James, when he called at the Cockburn Corner Drug Store for his daily newspaper, would linger in the back room. Several residents would join him. The summer colony of Western tycoons supplied a few regulars. The gossip was lively. James usually led the conversation. His companions were fascinated and delighted by his high good humour and gay wit. Then, within the hour, he would return to his embattled home, behind the big fence, nine feet high.

But James Dunn in his search for quiet went beyond mere security from outside intrusion. He insisted also on quiet inside his domain—except when he felt like making a noise himself. He objected strongly and even violently to whistling in the house. A new cook who whistled while preparing the food had to go. James was equally infuriated by the rustling of a newspaper in his presence, even if he was making precisely the same noise himself. He demanded silence—and he got it too, not only in his own house where he could exercise a master's authority, but elsewhere as well.

He stayed for long at the Seigniory Club, Quebec. When the Canadian Women's Curling Club was holding a convention there, the curlers were cheerful and exuberant. James was indignant when he heard these lively women making a lot of noise in the corridor outside his suite. He burst out and shouted: "Go away! Hear my first blast against the monstrous regiment of women." They went.

The next morning, and indeed every morning, rising at six o'clock he would toss a ball the length of his sitting room, while his several little dogs scrambled after it. This game would be carried on for more than half an hour. Occupants of the apartment below often insisted on changing their quarters.

In making noise he was highly proficient—in his hatred of noise he was not always consistent.

At the Ritz Hotel in Paris the rooms were so noisy that Christofor expected an abrupt departure. However, James made no complaint at all. He explained that he liked the large rooms with the lofty ceilings. He also liked to stimulate his historic imagination by looking out over the famous Place Vendome. These, he said, were sufficient compensations for the noise.

The real reason for his tolerance of the noise was different. He was flattered to find himself in the most important suite in the hotel.

However, that was an exception. At Dayspring he insisted on privacy, quiet and solitude. In fact, he made surprisingly little use of Dayspring as a place for truly gracious hospitality. Yet all the means were there. In his cellars there was more champagne than he and his friends would have drunk in a lifetime. There was also an impressive collection of claret. He never could resist buying any lot of fine champagnes or Bordeaux that a dealer might offer to him.

He had few guests to enjoy his hospitality and share his good things. I think Christofor would have liked to entertain more. But she would ask only those friends who were completely agreeable to him. This narrowed the range. Entertainment at Dayspring was confined to a very few close companions. Even these did not come very often.

He was no more forthcoming with his neighbours. He disapproved of some of them and, in fact, disapproved so strongly of his nearest neighbour that he would not even exchange a "How d'you do?".

A good mood! A bad mood! Both characteristic of James Dunn. By nature he was immensely hospitable. He loved lively company, especially the company of prominent people. He would listen attentively to their views on many matters.

Strange then that at Dayspring he should have surrounded himself with every luxury only to live almost like a recluse. His wife Christofor was of course his constant companion. His letters and messages, in writing and by telephone, his poems and remembrances, form an unbroken record of deep and abiding devotion to her which never faltered.

On June 2, 1947, Christofor had gone into hospital in Toronto. James wrote to her from an hotel:

"My darling Christofor,

I sit here trying to collect my thoughts to put into words my love and adoration of you. If anything injures you I feel the blow, if anything grieves you I suffer with you, I too am grieved, if you had to leave the world first I could not stay behind. I believe in the survival of the individual, the personal continuance of each one of us who wants to go on afterwards and my continual heaven is to go on with you, my Hell would be here or there without you. I must always keep step with you, never let you go anywhere without me, whatever the day months or years are that we are to go here, the time will be all too short. It is a dream of joy I cannot bear at any time to wake from, I worship you, your great spirit inhabits my soul and guides you to my best service.

Jimmy"

In the next month on the 27th of July he wrote to Christofor from Algoma: "Darling, This day of the year is the day on which was born the only real joy and co-operation and all other good things that I have had in my life. In all things and at all times, I have always found you loyally at my side. I offer you deep affection, admiration and always respect.

JIMMY"

They had intended to celebrate the birthday in New York. But the visit was deferred. Christofor was not free from tasks and duties when staying at the Waldorf Towers. She cooked his breakfast and served it herself in the dining room of their spacious quarters. Their lunch, consisting of egg or cheese dishes, was meticulously prepared in the cramped kitchen of the apartment and served by Christofor. Gracious living was sacrificed to long living.

The suite in New York and the entertaining arrangements at the Pavillon Restaurant were all paid for by Algoma. This was according to general practice and well-worn custom among American and Canadian business concerns.

At the Pavillon Restaurant gracious living came fully into its own. Dinner was a ceremonial occasion. Always sitting at the same table, James would be served with carefully selected and specially prepared foods under the personal supervision of the proprietor himself. He would drink one bottle of champagne and Christofor

To James Dunn
from his friend of many years
Winston S. Churchill

Warm regards to my friend Sir James Dunn

C. D. Howe

would have a bottle of claret. Tips to waiters and gratuities were out of all proportion to the common practice.

If James Dunn was not consistent in his pursuit of gracious living, he was also inconsistent in many other directions.

He was like a ship sailing the seas with a port light and a starboard light ablaze. On the port side there was immense generosity, kindliness and ready sympathy. There was humour, brilliant talk and charm. There was a pleasing and attractive countenance. On the starboard side there was at times a harsh appearance and an unsympathetic and even critical attitude to his friends and others. There was also a total indifference to public opinion.

Yet in spite of that indifference James was a man who greatly wanted to be liked. Perhaps he wanted to be liked on his own terms.

And in spite of his inconsistencies and eccentricities he won rewarding friendships in ample measure.

In one respect, he was certainly not indifferent to public opinion, and that was his dress. He was fastidious, almost to the point of dandyism. It was a curious foible in one who often seemed to insist on the roughness and severity of his manner.

But clothes were one of the ways in which he chose to enjoy his wealth—clothes after the double standard imposed by Beau Brummell, who laid down that dress should be perfect and also unobtrusive.

James Dunn lived up to these standards. Very often his tie, shirt, and suit would be of the one colour, but never a striking colour. He wore broad satin neckties, different in cut from the ordinary necktie and made for him in London.

He bought shirts and underwear on every visit to England. With a touch of vanity he would respond to comments on his small feet. His shoes were made in New York. Shoe-laces of the ribbon type were always ironed before use. He insisted on having elastic-top socks, so that they would not wrinkle over his ankles!

Although in the ordinary way he wore no hat even in winter, when posing for photographs he seldom failed to put one on. The reason for this idiosyncrasy was his desire to be a "North American" citizen, firmly supporting Canadian nationalism. "Englishmen," he said, "would not wear hats." He did not mean to be mistaken for an Englishman merely because he had lived there for thirty years.

Up-to-the-minute though James Dunn was in many ways, he was curiously old-fashioned in others. He never shaved with anything other than an open blade. And even when travelling in a swaying railway carriage, he managed to shave without cutting himself. He refused to use any safety type.

His hatred of the electric razor gave rise to a strange though typical outburst. Michael Wardell, visiting at Dayspring, was happily shaving himself. James, hearing the noise of the motor, rushed into the room, crying: "Stop, stop!"

Wardell turned to him in astonishment and was told by James that the air was being filled with little bits of hair—his stubble—which when breathed into the lungs would do incredible damage and might promote cancer.

Thereafter, when at Dayspring, Wardell never used his electric razor, wishing only that a silent type might be speedily invented.

As for hair-cutting, James would never consent to the barber using his own equipment. Dunn invariably carried with him a bag of hair-cutting implements and insisted on the operation being carried out by a Montreal French-speaking Canadian. James regularly brought the man from Montreal to St. Andrews for a hair-cut. The distance is five hundred miles.

In all matters concerning his appearance and his health he went his own way throughout his long life, using pure salt as his tooth powder and abhorring every form of medication. As for sleeping draughts, he had no need of them. He slept most afternoons, unless he had occasion to speak on the telephone. Like the Mohammedans, who prefer prayer to sleep, he preferred the telephone to sleep.

James was a great traveller. His motor cars were always on the go. Two Company airplanes, with crews standing permanently by, would fly him whenever and wherever the mood took him.

One named Victoria was his favourite chariot
and made much mileage throughout Canada,
with many journeys to New York and Virginia.

To make a journey when bad weather pre-
vented flying, he would charter a railway carriage from the Canadian Pacific Railway with as
little thought as another man might give to
buying a railway ticket.

His second Canadian house was a home in the
woods, a few miles outside his birthplace of
Bathurst. It was modestly called Dunn's Camp,
although the property actually covered more than
10,000 acres, bought from the Provincial Government.

It was not an expensive purchase and it certainly gave him an enormous amount of pleasure.

In the woods, he built a substantial house in
the Canadian style: walls of deal, shingled roof—
looking out upon a long and deep lake. A large
sitting-room with a view over the lake was called
Beaver Hall.

Life at the Camp was very far from fulfilling
Dunn's ideal of gracious living. Indeed, it was
positively ungracious. Nothing seemed to work
properly, not even the telephone. His struggles
with it were a trial to the temper of a man who
did not like being tried. The defective telephone
was a serious handicap, for he needed to keep in
continual contact with his business affairs.

The water supply was also unreliable. I remember one visit to the Camp with Jack Bickell
and Brendan Bracken. The pump broke down.

This did not distress the rest of us. We had a whole lake for bathing and an excellent cellar for drinking. But the disaster angered James Dunn so much that he took to a canoe and paddled up the lake by himself to work off his temper by solitary exercise.

The food was not good. It could hardly be, for there was only one road connecting the Camp with civilization, and that was a penance to ride over. Life at the Camp was fairly primitive. I enjoyed it.

In July 1944 I was in Washington attending meetings of the Allied Oil Committees. C. D. Howe and I set out for Canada. I suggested a stop over at Dunn's Camp, where James was in residence. We arrived on a Sunday morning. It was a happy occasion. James was determined to make Howe's visit a memorable event. And Howe was showing evidence of growing friendship and confidence which ultimately developed into close intimacy.

Dunn's Camp was a place of friendship, good company, excellent drink and stimulating conversation. The gravest disadvantage was not primitive discomfort but the danger from forest fires. There were several fires during the period of Dunn's occupancy, one of them very severe. The byres were burned down and the herd of milk cows was destroyed. Dunn was at Algoma. But by telephone he directed the operations. The Mounted Police who had arrived on the scene rejected these directions. Christofor was torn

between loyalty to her husband and respect for
two Mounties equipped with shooting arms.

Christofor sold the Camp in 1957. It is now
a tree farm.

I have always thought that the habit of spending some part of every year in a Camp constantly
threatened with fire was responsible for one of
James Dunn's idiosyncrasies. By nature, he was
fearless. He became an enthusiastic flyer at a
time when flying was still a novelty and regarded by many as a far too dangerous novelty.
He would sit beside the pilot enjoying the speed,
the height and the far horizons. Indifferent to
the dangers of a crash, a mechanical failure or
lost direction, there was still one thing he would
never allow. He would never permit the heating
to be switched on.

This was through his fear of fire. He could
not be persuaded that heating in an airplane was
no more dangerous than domestic heating—in
fact less so. On this question he would not listen
to reason. Even the pilot in the cockpit flying at
high altitudes in low temperatures was denied
the comfort of any heat at all. This phobia had
its most striking expression in a flight undertaken by James when he was eighty-one. He
took off from Sault Ste Marie when the ground
temperature was sub-zero. James was heavily
wrapped up and, as always, refused to have the
heating turned on, in spite of all arguments and
pleas. The plane flew at twelve thousand feet
and became as cold within as an icicle. At jour-

ney's end in New Brunswick, James was quite comfortable. But his fellow-passenger had to spend a week in bed.

Fear of fire was not his only anxiety complex. Fear of burglars, fear of night marauders and intruders, ruled his latter years. Gates, doors and windows were barred and bolted. If awakened in the night he would ask if security measures had been properly carried out.

He was never alone by day or night. His insistence on companionship did not necessarily call for conversation. He was quite willing to read or write letters in silence, providing only that he was not unattended.

This curious habit of fear of fire, of burglars, and of solitude, in one so bold and brave in all his attitudes, left behind him a legacy which has been inherited by those who shared the intimacy of his daily routine.

His apartment in the Waldorf Towers was like an ancient keep. The doors were double locked and a chain was always in use. When visitors applied for admission the door on the chain gave security. The identity of applicants disposed of, entrance was permitted.

His own method of gaining entry was something in the nature of a password. He would ring the bell seven times, two long, three short and two longer summons, would bring immediate response. No chains needed.

Barbara, the maid, when doing the rooms during James's absence, was instructed to brush the carpet at the entrance while walking back-wards. Thus any intruder would be betrayed by his footprints. On one occasion Mr. Dell'Agnese, the hotel manager, used his pass key to deliver flowers that had been sent to Lady Dunn. James saw on returning the tell-tale footprints but not the flowers. A storm broke out which subsided with explanations.

The hotel staffs liked James just as his per-sonal servants were devoted to him. Dell'Agnese, who endured much, speaks of him to this day with marked affection. And Barbara, the maid, always said: "A genius must behave like that."

Skinner, his valet for so many years, always showed his complete admiration for James's dominating ways and in conversation with others invariably called him the King of Kak-i-ak.

It may be right to mention here that James was a constant and untiring reader of Erle Stan-ley Gardner's detective stories.

The restless energy of the man found expres-sion in constant travel. Christofor was his quar-termaster-general on these journeys, carrying all that he deemed necessary in hat boxes. Some of these boxes were packed with cooking equip-ment, a small electric stove, an electric hot plate, an electric saucepan and so on. In others she carried boot-polishing material, for James at-tached great importance to his shoes being polished till they shone like glass. Sometimes he would discard as many as five pairs of shoes before he found a pair polished to his liking.

Still more hat boxes carried specially prepared food, packages of specially blended teas, pots of honey and glucose and molasses.

One item was too big for a hat box: the twenty-one pounds of special cereal prepared for James by the Midland Mills, Ontario. This was carried around in a small sack, and cost considerable excess baggage fees at every airport.

James Dunn was swept by enthusiasm for different kinds of diet as the ocean is swept by the tropical storm. The storm, did not, as a rule, last for long.

Once, when he was travelling on the midnight train from London to Glasgow for an important meeting in Kelvin Hall of the British Celanese Company which he and Loewenstein had financed, his secretary, Sims, was travelling with him. James invited Sims to have breakfast.

Without asking Sims what he might wish to eat, he directed the steward to bring two large plates of porridge.

Sims said, rather diffidently: "Only one, steward, I don't take porridge."

James ignored this and repeated: "*Two* plates of your wonderful Scots porridge, steward."

Sims again murmured: "Only one, steward."

At this James turned upon him and roared: "What in hell *do* you eat?"

Sims replied that he would like eggs and bacon.

"Eggs are all right," James agreed grudgingly, "but bacon isn't worth a hoot in hell!"

Then feeling that he had been harsh to his faithful secretary, Dunn presented him, quite unexpectedly, with a magnificent present for his wife.

At one time he liked raw vegetables and hated red meat. His meals during this phase would consist of potatoes cooked in their jackets, bread baked with Canadian flour, and fresh green vegetables and fruit.

Then he tired of this fare. Lord Castlerosse, his close friend, noted in his column in the *Sunday Express* that he had watched this supposed vegetarian eat "a huge plate of roast beef".

He reported that after each mouthful Dunn would pause to condemn all vegetarians.

Dunn's pursuit of these food fantasies was, in fact, altogether lacking in consistency. For instance, he would refuse to eat anything at dinner. Then by eleven or twelve o'clock at night he would eat twice as much—or more—than would have satisfied him at dinner. This was his idea of following a diet.

Dunn then had a spell during which he added brewer's yeast and wheat germ to everything he ate. He would lecture his friends on the benefits of Yoga and breathing exercises.

Yet again, he would take a teaspoonful of raw cod liver oil every morning, and eat honey instead of sugar. He was convinced, during this phase, that sugar was bad for human beings.

He took to swallowing a preparation composed of garlic and charcoal, which he claimed cleansed and purified the whole alimentary tract. He said, too, it was good for the arteries. It certainly was not good to the taste.

When he was in New Brunswick at the right season, fresh blueberries with honey supplanted other food fancies. He would chew the resin gathered from the spruce trees, declaring that this gum also cleansed and purified the alimentary tract. Asked why he chose this curious diet, his answer was decisive: "Blueberries and honey —the food of bears; spruce resin their delicacy."

Fresh fish was another fancy with him. So determined was he in his passion that the fish must be really fresh, that he took to appearing on the beach when the catch was brought in. Thus there might be no doubt that he was being served with fish just out of the sea.

One morning, his fisherman returned late and James, tired of waiting, went back to the house he was at that time occupying at Hythe. But not for long. He came back unexpectedly and unobserved, just in time to see his fisherman gathering some herrings from a Mac Fisheries Box, placing them in salt water and parcelling them for delivery to his customer, James Dunn.

This experience influenced his selection of foods for many a day. The search for fresh fish resembled henceforth an Erle Stanley Gardner detective story.

When James was at home, his principal meal occurred in the middle of the day, for every evening he insisted on having rice to eat. He was sure that rice controlled blood pressure. As his own blood pressure was measured every day, first by the left arm and then by the right, the result also served as a check on rice diet. A small machine for this purpose was carried always and on every journey in a special box.

So it is fair to say that Dunn took a deep interest in all varieties of dietary practices. He discussed food values with friends and even acquaintances.

James would often deny himself the pleasures of good food at my house, but he never turned away from good drink. His taste in champagne was wonderfully well developed. And he would pass sound judgment on claret and brandy.

At home, Dunn would have a glass of whisky before lunch, and another before dinner. When he was away from home, he would drink a whole bottle of champagne every night.

Scotch whisky was always a favourite drink with him. He was frequently intolerant of those who rejected his splendid wines and sometimes too outspoken in his denunciation of teetotallers.

He would often chaff his very dear friend Lord Greenwood, a teetotal Canadian (from Whitby, Ontario), who had been a professional temperance lecturer. Greenwood found favour with a Liberal constituency and gained a seat in Parliament. He was an orator with fixed political views, and noted for his platform repartee. His accent gave the impression that he was speaking through his nose. When an opponent at a public

meeting, who supported tariffs against foreigners, cried out: "You speak through your
nose," Greenwood answered: "If you get tariffs,
you will pay through your nose."

Under Lloyd George he was appointed Secretary of State for Ireland. His administration,
although denounced by all Ireland and many of
his Liberal Party Colleagues, was a most impressive success. And his courage and devotion
to duty in the face of threats of assassination
won him credit and high praise.

James Dunn admired and liked Greenwood.

However, he would not yield to James's banter
on the subject of liquor. His teetotal habits prevailed.

Fascination with the subject of food and drink
stayed with James Dunn all through his life.
His interest persisted through the years. In the
1940's, as twenty years earlier, he would still
devote a vast amount of thought and energy to
making sure that his food was totally pure and
prepared as he wished it. While staying for the
last time at the Ritz in Paris he refused his
porridge, saying that the milk was stale and not
properly pasteurized and therefore not fit for
human consumption.

Christofor declared that she was sure it had
been pasteurized, but he retorted that, even if
this were so, pasteurization would not make stale
milk fresh.

At dawn next morning, James, carrying his
own container, was driven through the outskirts

of Paris until he reached the fields. When he saw a good-looking farm-house with a big barn which he thought would be sheltering cows, he stopped the car.

He knocked at the door and explained that he wanted to buy milk and would pay well for it if the cow could be milked directly into his own receptacle.

He carried the basin of milk back to the Ritz, where Christofor went through some process which he described as pasteurization. Then he sat down and agreed to eat his porridge. He said the milk was delicious. The journey into the country was repeated every morning.

While at sea, he drank a glass of ocean water every day. A steward was required to gather the water from the ship's bow, contrary to the usual practice of collecting it from the stern. James would often supervise the collection of his beverage in the interests of sanitation.

He was always suspicious that his health might be affected by the wrong food treated in the wrong way. When he sailed from New York to Southampton in a strange liner, not a Cunard vessel, he had grievances on the first day out. He claimed the blankets were made of some form of fibre glass and were disagreeable to him.

This provoked alarm in his mind about what he was being given to eat. He visited the kitchens. What he saw did not dispel his fears.

Fish was being cooked on a production line where the chef held a hot swatter, and attacked every piece of fish with it to give the impression that the cooking had been done on a grill, when, in fact, it had been cooked by electricity.

In Dunn's view, all the food on the ship was electrocuted. For the rest of the journey he would eat nothing but honeydew melons and yoghourt. He had five days of this restricted diet.

He was a master of games of chance and skill which he practiced as a distraction from his business affairs. Backgammon, chequers and gin rummy were favourites with him. Intense concentration and a competitive spirit explained his high average of success.

At golf his success was one hundred per cent, for he played a game of his own which he could not possibly lose.

Two partners took turns at playing the same ball. Thus, Dunn could not be outdriven. Needless to say, his partner was Christofor. Even this individual form of golf was abandoned when steel clubs came in. James could not break a steel club when he was enraged by a bad shot. That was the end of golf.

Although with his enormous wealth and his attractive love of life he could command most things, sometimes he met defeat.

For several years James would not go to London. His dispute with the British Income Tax, referred to on page 147, had reached a stage where legal action was threatened, and James was convinced that he would be at a disadvantage in negotiating a settlement if he submitted him-

self to the jurisdiction of the British Courts. He
made Paris his European headquarters and it
was while staying there that he telephoned his
friend S. W. Alexander, at one time an editor
on the *Express* staff. "Come to Paris," he said,
"and stay with me for a few days."

Alexander, who owns and edits the *City
Press*, accepted this pleasing proposal. But there
was such a shortage of seats on airplanes, with
so many officials travelling to and fro, that he
could not book a plane. He regretfully rang Dunn
to turn down the invitation.

"We are going to Drumoland Castle in Ireland tomorrow," James replied. "Come over
and see us there. If you cannot get a seat on a
plane, charter one. Ring up Croydon airport
and book a plane for Sunday morning."

Alexander tells what followed:

"I did just that, left Croydon in solitary state
in a 12-seater aircraft, and arrived at Shannon
soon after eleven.

"There a car was waiting to take me to
Drumoland. When I arrived James was standing
at the top of the staircase holding out his hand.
If I remember, a curtain was pulled and in the
centre was his young wife.

"Turning to her he said: 'And now I want
to introduce you to your little friend again.'

"He had gone to an enormous amount of
trouble."

But this Irish stay, though delightful for my
friend Alexander, ended unfortunately for Dunn.

LADY DUNN   Salvador Dali
"James's favourite portrait."

Bad weather delayed his departure for eight days and nights; the Dunns were storm-stayed. James in a fever of impatience was beyond restraint. He criticized everything that was Irish. Daily he made an excursion to Limerick, claiming that his need for food could only be satisfied by crackers and cheese at a local grocery shop. When at last the storm blew away, James without a moment's delay flew to his Canadian home. In attendance was Christofor, quartermaster-general with the pots and pans, tea leaves, oatmeal and honey and the boot-polishing material.

James never visited Ireland again.

Chapter 15

DREAMER OF DREAMS

It is through Art and through Art only,
that we can realize our perfection.
                                        —WILDE

How FORTUNATE IS the man who possesses some ruling passion in which he can find refuge from the harsh struggles of life! James Dunn had this good fortune: he loved paintings with ardour and an instructed perception. Rich men have assembled striking collections on their walls. Dunn did something more than that: he made two collections, the first, small but of extraordinary quality, the second a fine and individual gathering of art, yet quite different in character from the first.

Quite early in his career, he began to take an interest in pictures. It reflected the spiritual side of his nature, a side which was so attractive to his friends. This had nothing at all to do with the harsh, stern duty of managing Algoma or of great financial enterprises. On that account, it was all the more refreshing and endearing.

Dunn's purchases began when he first had money to spare, possibly in 1908. Sir William

Van Horne, Chairman and President of the Canadian Pacific Railway, advised and influenced him in this early awakening of interest.

Van Horne was himself a competent artist; in the Montreal Gallery there hangs a single example from his brush—a painting of a steel works so realistic that one feels the frame must be a window in the wall opening on the vast panorama of chimneys, cranes, and furnaces.

This great art collector, Van Horne, was a sturdy, short and stout man with a beard, and the heaviest smoker of cigars I have ever known, not excluding Churchill.

Just how much he depended on cigars I did not realize until he carried me in his private railway carriage from New York to Montreal. It was long ago. He wanted me to take over the electric light system in Demerara, then under his charge. We met in the Grand Central waiting-room. Van Horne's valet, in charge of the baggage, was delayed.

As we talked, he offered me a cigar. I lit up. This unhappily was the only one he carried on him, and I realized that I had deprived him of it. He became so nervous and agitated that he forgot about the electric light plant, while I blurted out words of regret over my stupidity.

Then his servant arrived.

"Cigars! Cigars!" cried Sir William.

A box was produced. He ripped it open and in his haste spilled some cigars over the floor. After that he calmed down, and on the journey north we completed the deal over the Demerara company.

Van Horne, the greatest railway pioneer in Canada, had a rival, James J. Hill, who built the Great Northern Railway, through the American West. The two men fell out, and, in due course, their quarrel became well known to the public. Naturally, during that journey to Montreal, I asked Van Horne about his rival. He told me that Hill was a very fine man, honest and diligent. He would even choose Hill to be an executor of his estate, confident in the knowledge that every dollar would reach his wife and family—except, he added sharply, "except for the railways. He'd steal every damn one of them!"

Sir William gave Montreal Fine Arts Gallery their finest collection of pictures. Long before the First World War—on December 27, 1911—he wrote to Dunn:

"I am very glad to hear of your purchase of that magnificent Jacob Maris.

"I am sure you will never regret it, for I feel sure that it will some day rank as one of the half dozen world's masterpieces in landscape, and be spoken of with Rembrandt's Mill and Vermeer's View of Delft.

"It is better to buy one such picture than a hundred average things. A half dozen of that class will in themselves make a famous collection.

"I hope you will stick to the 'top notchers' and keep your eyes shut to the second class.

Two such great things quite fill a room. They need space and it is a sin to force inferior company upon them.

"I should very much like to have a photograph of your three Goyas if you should at any time have them to spare."

This was wise advice to a young collector from one who spent much time and taste on the purchase of works of art. "Keep your eyes shut to the second class." Dunn amassed his fine art collection on that sound principle.

A picture by Maris was a wise choice on his part. The work of this artist is so highly thought of today that twelve of his paintings are now in the National Gallery.

On April 5, 1912, Van Horne wrote Dunn urging him to purchase "a little sketch head" by Velasquez. He thought the sum asked of £20,000 was "more than absurd" and recommended an offer at a greatly reduced price.

Sir William also referred to a report that Altman, a New York collector, paid one million dollars for two Velasquez paintings, but he ridiculed it.

When the Fischer trouble overwhelmed Dunn, the bitterest blow was the dispersal of his collection. He sold several of his beloved paintings to Knoedlers, the art dealers, for £80,000. They wrote on July 28, 1914:

"Dear Dunn,

"I enclose cheque value £25,000, and con-

firm the purchase by us of your collection of
pictures for £80,000 as follows:—

Holbein	"Pt. of Queen Catherine Howard"
Memling	"Pt. of a Young Man"
Bronzino	"Pt. of Francisco de Medici"
Gainsborough	"Pt. of Mrs. Fitzherbert"
J. Maris	"The Bridge"
Goya	"Pt. of the Marquis de Castro Terreno"
Goya	"Pt. of the Marquisade Castro Terreno"
Goya	"Pt. of a Lady"
Ruysdael	"View of Haarlem"
El Greco	"An Apostle"
Manet	"Bull Fighters"
Stevens	"Waiting"
H. Met de	"A Saint"
Bles	" do. "

"We herewith agree to take care of the bill of
£30,000 due August 30th, £10,000 due October 13th, and £10,000 due January 13th, 1915.
The balance of £5,000 will be put to the credit
of your account, which I will make up and let
you know about later."

Holbein, Memling, Ruysdael, Goya—it was
indeed a collection of splendour! And Knoedlers
did not get everything. About the same time,
Dunn sold some of his paintings to Henry Clay
Frick. These masterpieces are now exhibited in
the matchless Frick Collection, New York. The

Director of the Collection has given this information:

"It appears that the following paintings were formerly owned by Sir James Dunn, in the order of the dates they were acquired:

February 28th 1914—*Gainsborough*—A portrait of Lady Innes.

February 28th 1914—*Hogarth*—A portrait of Miss Mary Edwards.

December 5th 1914—*Goya*—A Portrait of Dona Maria Martinez de Puga.

December 5th 1914—*Manet*—a Bull Fight.*

November 27th 1915—*Bronzino*—A Portrait of a Young Man."†

The paintings that went to Frick would of course be worth today many times the prices Dunn must have received in 1914 and 1915—of which there is no record.

I know what sadness overwhelmed him as he took down from the walls of his home one after another of these pictures he treasured. But it was never his way to grieve over what could not be remedied. While he dispersed that wonderful first collection, James Dunn resolved that one day he would buy even finer pictures. His fancy turned for a time to the work of contemporary artists, and at the end of the war he began once more to buy.

---

* This is a portion of a painting by Manet which was cut into two by some unknown person. James Dunn owned both pictures. He sold the other, "Bull Fighters", to Knoedlers in 1914.

† Not to be confused with the Portrait of Francisco de Medici by Bronzino which James sold to Knoedlers.

In the early days of his financial recovery after the Fischer default, his first choice may have been a picture named "Dorelia" painted by Augustus John. This beautiful product of John's genius was for many years hanging in the dining room at Dunn's London home, where he could see it every time he sat down to eat.

When the war of 1939 came ten years later, James was in Canada. He gave "Dorelia" to his second wife. The days and months and years rolled by, and one afternoon I bought it for just short of £5,000. Its value had multiplied rapidly, but not as swiftly as the stock of Algoma!

Another picture by John, named "Dodo", showed a woman dressed in a flowing and dark garment, with her hair loose and wild, carrying a staff and surrounded by flowers. I have searched for this portrait, but cannot find any trace of it, though a sketch of "Dodo" was recently shown to me.

By mid-February 1929, John was engaged in painting a family group with James wearing a blue shirt, fashioned as a coat.

Another artist to benefit from Dunn's lavish patronage was Sir William Orpen, who was directed to paint seventeen portraits of famous politicians and generals attending the Versailles Peace Conference. One thousand pounds each was the price, with sketches thrown in.

In May, 1919, James made friends with a future Vice-President of the United States, General Dawes. Writing to the General in Paris,

Dunn described Pershing, who commanded the U.S. Army in France, as a "courteous and charming General, and certainly a fine-looking soldier."

"In this connection," he added, "please try and see that he gives time to Orpen for a sitting. I do not think there is any question that Orpen is the greatest portrait painter of the day, with the possible exception of Sargent.

"One has to go back to the period of Gainsborough to find anything in English art comparing with Orpen's best work."

Strange over-valuation of Orpen. But history may prove that Dunn had a little of justification, for there are fashions in paintings as there are in women's clothes.

Pershing was persuaded to go to Orpen's studio. But not for long. The sittings were few and brief. When Orpen asked for "three more minutes", Pershing replied: "Three minutes! I decided to fight some of the greatest battles in this war in three minutes."

When Dunn was created a baronet in 1921 for his wartime services, Orpen wrote to him in verse:

"I am delighted, Sir, to get
    The news you are a Baronet.
    No titles can increase the fame
    Of your already glorious name,
    But I am thankful that the King
    Has had them do the proper thing:
        Congratulations, Sir, From your
            devoted servant, William Orpen."

In his dealings with Orpen, James Dunn's un-
canny sense of values for once deserted him.
His Orpen pictures went down in value.

Five years later, on July 16, 1926, he sold
these pictures at Christie's—36 portraits and
sketches that Orpen had done of delegates to the
Versailles Peace Conference. James had paid
£17,500 for the paintings and expenses. He
sold the lot for £13,497.

They were not sold as a collection, but separately. The highest price was £2,730 for the
portrait of President Wilson; the lowest, £95,
for the sketch of George Barnes, the British
Labour Representative to the Versailles Conference. Pershing's picture fetched £525.

Of many other pictures that Dunn commis-
sioned from Orpen, only two now remain. One
is of his colleague Loewenstein, who died so
strangely over the English Channel, and the
other is of Mona, James Dunn's beloved daughter. Both are very fine examples of the painter's
work.

Then came a period when Dunn bought many
of Sir Alfred Munnings's pictures. This phase
was short-lived, because Dunn met Sickert and
was immediately drawn to this brilliant man,
with his charming, casual, easy-going way of
life.

Sickert was living in a small tumble-down
house on the edge of London when Dunn bought
two of his small paintings, which he gave to
friends.

By 1932 in the depth of the depression, when industrial and financial conditions were very serious, Sickert was in low estate, for few people could afford to buy paintings.

Dunn, anxious to help so distinguished an artist, and with the intention of giving him comfort and joy at a time of gloom, agreed to buy twelve paintings. Dunn would choose the subjects himself. He wanted twelve portraits of his friends.

Dunn arranged to pay Sickert £250 for each picture. There was to be one portrait of Lord Greenwood, one of Lord Castlerosse, and three of James, one of Christofor, then his secretary, and afterwards his third wife, and one of me, which is now built into the structure of the *Daily Express* office in Manchester.

Although such a prudent man of business, James generously paid Sickert the money before getting possession of the pictures. Thereafter Sickert was slow in delivering these canvases and, indeed, left London without telling James of his intention to do so.

He was next discovered at St. Peter's, Thanet, in Kent. James pursued him there with some haste to ask for his pictures. He was directed to Sickert's house and knocked. There was no bell.

The front door was opened, and, very cautiously, Sickert looked out. When he saw James, he slammed it shut again, crying: "Go away! I'm not at home!"

Christofor thereafter undertook to visit Sickert. She succeeded in making an entry into his home, took photographs of his unfinished portraits, and brought back two of his nearly completed works strapped to the side of her car.

About this time I invited Sickert to a party at Stornoway House. In his inconsequential way, he arrived with his wife by taxi-cab from Thanet, a distance of probably 60 miles. The meter on the cab ticked on through the night. When the party came to an end—at about four or five o'clock the following morning—the meter was still ticking.

By that time the bill was considerable.

When the time came for Sickert to return home, the taxi-driver, who knew him of old, insisted on payment, not only for the journey up from Thanet, but also for the journey back again, before he would leave.

After much argument, a friend of Sickert's paid the man, but on the way to the coast the taxi ran into a telegraph pole, and Sickert and his wife were badly shaken. Luckily, no one was seriously injured.

Dunn never took an interest in Canadian painters. He always held that the work of Canadian artists was of inferior quality, and altogether too much influenced by various schools of art, to be classed with the pictures of his choice. Despite this oft-expressed opinion, he had his portrait painted by the artist Alphonse Jongers, resident in Canada, often described as a French-speaking Canadian but in fact a native of France. James sat for it at the Camp and he liked it very much. I do, too.

None the less, Dunn continually criticized and objected to my selection of Canadian paintings. He did not approve of Krieghoff. He regarded this artist's work as of historical value, as part of the social history of the Province of Quebec. But, he declared, Krieghoff has little merit as a painter.

Dunn had certain strong preferences in colours. His favourites were blue and yellow, he disliked brown. He considered that it lacked distinction.*

He was annoyed when Sickert, on his commission, painted Lord Castlerosse in brown: he rejected the portrait. The artist and his model joined in arguing that the colour was in fact cinnamon. Together, they persuaded James.

It was the love of brightness and gaiety that attracted him to Salvador Dali.

In the autumn of 1947, James was dining in the Pavillon Restaurant in New York. Sitting opposite was a man with a fierce exotic face with antler-shaped black mustachios all a'quiver and eyes almost shooting sparks with the absorbed intensity of their gaze. He was watching James, who tried to ignore this trance-like image with his chin resting on a very thin peculiar-looking stick with a jewelled crook.

---

* The Marquis of Curzon said "Gentlemen never wear brown."

By the time the fruit course was reached the Proprietor, Soulé, came to James bearing a card and offering excuses for the intrusion.

He whispered softly that the Great Dali desired to be presented forthwith.

James with hands clasped over his plate of sectioned pear was quite entranced with what he was hearing—he smacked his hands together and in ringing tones, that certainly were intended to reach the image opposite, declared: "Grand. Splendid. I am intrigued to meet him."

Dali leaped from his place on the banquette before Soulé could even turn round, and sat himself almost on top of James, who was rubbing his hands together in schoolboyish glee.

"Caesar." Dali cried. "The countenance, the bone formation of Caesar—Augustus Caesar. You are a Roman."

"No." replied James with a note of pride. "I am of Irish descent."

"No, no." said Dali. "Twice no. The Irish have little culture. They have no knowledge of my pictures. I am a believer in reincarnation and I am sure you are descended from the Great Caesar."

James was on the verge of resenting the attack on Ireland and for a moment the alliance between the two showmen might have been strangled at birth. But Dali escaped from the impending crisis by asking for an account of James's parents, his training, his education and his interest in books and art.

James was telling "the story of his birth", with a detailed record of his collection of paintings. Dali with a gesture of impatience said: "We are discussing art, not commercial illustrations. Filippo Lippi, that was a Great Master; Vermeer and Zurbaran, they are immortal."

James made no defence of his Sickerts, Orpens and Johns. Asked about his reading habits, he said: "I read biographies of the leaders through the centuries. Caesar—Augustus Caesar —Genghis Khan, Suleiman, Alexander and Napoleon."

"My favourite subjects," shouted Dali showing enthusiasm and excitement. "They carved out their Empires. They conquered vast domains. I have conquered the whole world of art."

James, somewhat disturbed by Dali's monopoly of the conversation, plunged into an account of Algoma. Dali was not listening though pretending to be interested.

Suddenly another crisis.

James, mentioning Algoma and not for the first time, was asked by the Master: "What's Algoma? A new vegetable?"

The Algoma treatise came to an abrupt conclusion. The Master recovered the lost ground by discussing the bone formation of James's hands and feet. Peace and amity were restored.

Naturally, Dali, who was staying at the St. Regis Hotel, visited James at the Waldorf by invitation early next morning and began a series of sittings lasting over many days.

Dali's studio set up in wartime was at Pebble Beach, California. He hastily arranged accommodation for James and Christofor at a Club near by. When it was revealed that a rule of 'No dogs' prevailed, James, who travelled with a little pinscher named Alexander, sent a telegramme to Dali: "If Caesar cannot bring Alexander to Cyprus arrangements must be abandoned." Dali telegraphed in reply: "Caesar may bring his angel I await arrivals with great passion."

The Dunns and their dog travelled West in the airplane *Victoria*.

A week of sittings exasperated James. His impatience was disturbing the calm of the studio. Then the formality of unveiling the canvas. James on a throne wearing a golden-satin toga and in bare feet; Dali expectant, his wife standing near by paying no attention to the picture but looking at her husband with adoration.

James and Christofor were stunned. They gazed on the scene in silence. At last the quiet was shattered. James gave a great loud long almost howling laugh, clapping his hands over and over, by no means a demonstration of applause.

Dali with dampened spirits asked for judgment. James replied: "Give me time."

No more was said. The picture was taken to the Waldorf Towers in New York. Christofor, deciding to ban its exhibition, hung the masterpiece in her own bedroom.

Meanwhile Chandor, an American portrait painter who had gained the distinction of a commission from the Queen, painted a portrait of James (price $9,000). This work of art was hanging prominently in the dining room.

Dali and Chandor were asked to attend a Sunday afternoon viewing of these masterpieces.

Chandor, admiring "James the Emperor" bowed low to Dali declaring: "The work of a Great Master."

Dali standing erect with haughty condescension replied: "You have painted a kindly old gentleman."

The party was over. The guests departed in separate lifts.

Some time afterwards, James and Christofor visited La Turbie in the South of France, where there is a famous statue of Augustus Caesar.

Seeing it, James at once recalled Dali's words and the portrait.

"I'll stand beside this statue," he told Christofor, "and you can take a photograph of Caesar and me together. Then I'll examine it and see whether Dali was right."

He posed by the base of the monument, but Christofor explained that she could not take a clear picture of both James and Augustus Caesar because the statue towered so high above that it was impossible for her to focus them together.

James immediately climbed up the monument

Author's Note: For the verbatim account of these conversations I am indebted to a contemporary record.

until he was standing shoulder to shoulder with Caesar, then his wife took the photograph.

When it was developed, Dunn agreed that Dali was right. He *was* like Caesar.

The Dali portrait of James in toga is now on view for the first time at the Beaverbrook Art Gallery in Fredericton.

Dali painted Christofor seated on a horse, with a falcon perched on her wrist. This was Dunn's favourite portrait. And it is indeed a wonderful work.

James's love of pictures certainly extended to a love of being portrayed. He enjoyed contacts with painters and admired their special talents. Conversations with artists always fascinated him. And these diversions gave him relief from the stresses and strains of his eventful and exciting business activities.

In just over forty years, fourteen portraits of James were painted. The list is as follows:

Harrington Mann	1916
Augustus John (three portraits)	1920s & 1930s
Sickert (two portraits)	1930s
Alphonse Jongers	1930s
Gerald Brockhurst	1940
Douglas Chandor	1947
Elmer Greene	1947
Henry Carr	1947
Dali (three portraits)	1948-1955

Fourteen portraits! I have always believed that Dunn had some resemblance in character to Bernard Shaw. This belief is strengthened by his passion for portraits and the patience he showed over and over again, in sitting for portrait painters.

Shaw's home, according to Wells, was adorned by more than fourteen portraits of the playwright. Wells said that if some archaeologist dug up Shaw's Corner in the distant future when our civilization had been forgotten, he would find so many busts of Shaw that he would believe he had come upon the shrine of some great god.

James Dunn did not go so far as Shaw, but he did have a self-regarding element in his nature. He liked recognition, and not only by portraiture. He was admitted to the bar of five different Canadian Provinces. As he had not the slightest intention of practising law, these admissions had no practical significance at all. But they pleased him. After all, law was his nominal profession, and he liked to be acknowledged by his brothers of the robe. Dunn was determined to impress himself. He also wanted to impress others.

As portrait painters, John and Sickert failed to please him. Yet, both John and Sickert portraits hanging in the Beaverbrook Art Gallery in Fredericton are praised by artists, critics and public.

Of John's other work for Dunn it is impossible to form any opinion. James destroyed a conversation piece. Two portraits were banished to the attic at Dayspring and have never been seen.

Dunn's quarrels with John over the various portraits were furious, and much tough language
was tossed to and fro, without reaching any conclusion. On one occasion, John spent several
weeks at James's villa Lomas at St. Jean Cap
Ferrat, making repeated attempts to please his
patron but always with disastrous results. John,
however, gave as much as he got.

Whenever James visited a city or capital in
America or abroad, his first leisure moments
were always given over to journeys to the picture galleries.

In New York, the Frick Gallery was James's
favourite, and he spent many hours there exam-
ining—among others—the paintings he had been
forced to sell in 1914 and 1915, when Fischer
defaulted.

He visited the National Gallery in Washington and the Louvre in Paris at every opportunity.

Such was his love of great paintings that he
willingly drove for nine hours to reach Basle
and then had a nine hours' motor journey back
to Paris—and this in his 77th year. He spent an
entire day at the Kunstmuseum, fascinated by
the collection of Holbeins.

To look closely at pictures he would take out
a pair of glasses from his breast pocket, inspect
the work, and then take them off for further
examination.

He would tell Christofor his own estimate of
the value of a picture, often stated in terms of

money. Frequently he would give her some interesting details about the artist and the scene. Vermeer, Holbein and Rembrandt were among his favourite painters.

Even though James has been dead now for some years his wise choice of pictures and his love of beautiful things live on in the magnificent gifts that the Sir James Dunn Foundation has given to the Beaverbrook Art Gallery in Fredericton.

Commanding one wall in the Central Gallery there is the monumental and controversial Dali, "Santiago El Grande" (Saint James the Great). This is a tremendous picture 13′6″ high by 10′ wide—a great blaze of blue, at which no one could look and remain indifferent.

It is a tribute to Spain's military patron saint; Dali shows the saint carrying the Cross upward on a rearing horse. The domelike background represents both a scallop shell (one of the symbols of Santiago) and what the artist calls "a whole cathedral surging from the waters". This picture is the favourite piece in the Gallery and commands immense attention from every section, young and old together. Many visitors sit for long looking in silence and profound meditation upon Santiago.

The Gallery also contains a portrait of James by Dali. It is Lady Dunn's favourite picture of her husband. It is called "Sunrise", and it is a striking, unusual study. The white hair and clean-cut features of James stand out clearly against a background of the same startling blue that was his favourite colour.

In the English Gallery there is one long wall with many paintings by Sickert. In the centre hangs his full-length portrait of Lord Castlerosse in a characteristic pose. He stands with his back to a fireplace, feet wide apart, his coat flowing, with his hands in his pockets. His eyes are closed and he is smiling like a cherub or even a seraph. The artist signed the canvas as at "St. Peter's, Thanet." Unusual for Sickert.

To the left of this painting hangs a full-length portrait of James Dunn—my favourite Sickert. True, there are defects, but the poise and attitude of the subject gives this portrait an importance and distinction that marks it as a great and abiding work of genius. To the right is an exciting picture of Edward VIII, when King, about to spring up a flight of steps, a detective hovering to his right.

This strange portrait of the King in the uniform of the Guards Brigade, wearing a mourning band of crepe, is the subject of close study and much comment.

Sickert may have foreseen the Abdication and the Marriage, when he grasped and reproduced the character of King Edward. Future writers about the romance of the Duke and Duchess of Windsor should look upon the artist's labours before undertaking their own tasks. Everything is explained and all is excused in a painting on a piece of canvas six feet by three.

Facing the portrait of Lord Castlerosse, across the width of three galleries, is "Dorelia" by Augustus John, the magnificent painting that gave James Dunn so much pleasure at Norwich House, and which after so many years I purchased from the Leicester Galleries in London.

Whenever I walk through this Gallery, with here and there the pictures of my friends, and the paintings they loved, I feel very close to James. It is as though something of his spirit also walks with me, in close companionship.

Chapter 16

ETERNITY

Now the day is over,
Night is drawing nigh.
Shadows of the evening
Steal across the sky.
　　　　　　　　—BARING-GOULD

IN THE CLOSING years of his life Dunn's astonishingly assimilative memory remained as clear and sharp as when he first attended the lectures of Professor Loisette.

He could still remember telephone numbers of friends and business acquaintances in many countries in an amazing way. Arriving at a strange town he would instruct his secretary to contact such a person, and give the number as well. He never had any need of address books or directories to help him.

On the telephone he talked so frequently that his manner was gruff and his conversation abrupt. To the usual enquiry about how he felt he would reply even as his health was failing: "Never felt better in all my life."

He was of course influenced by the teaching of Emile Coué, the French physician, who required his patients to say: "Every day, and in

every way, I am getting better and better."
Self-suggestion, it was held, would improve the
patient's condition. "Thinking makes it so."

He was intolerant when others made use of
abbreviations. The word "phone", instead of
"telephone", annoyed him unreasonably. He believed in maintaining high standards, and was
impatient with what he referred to as "lazy care-
lessness".

When I complimented him on his memory, he
said that the mind was like a crystal stream; one
should never allow it to slow down, but keep it
flowing clearly and swiftly. If one let it slacken,
then it would soon become cloudy and cluttered
up with useless things.

His vigour, like his memory, stayed with him
to the end.

When surrounded by congenial companions,
James Dunn would sit up as late at night as others
could be persuaded to keep him company.

On one occasion when Michael Wardell visited
him, he spent the whole night talking of his early
life, of incidents in his career, and of events relat-
ing to the development of Algoma.

Just at dawn, Wardell fell asleep. When he
wakened up later in the morning, he found that
James was asleep, too. They both went off to
bed much amused.

James liked Wardell and they saw much of
each other. In 1952, the British publisher sold
his London paper for £250,000. Just five years
earlier he had launched it with a total capital

amounting to £15,000. A profit of £235,000 on such a small investment in these few years was certainly remarkable.

Now Wardell's newspaper and other holdings in Fredericton, New Brunswick, Canada, represent an investment of nearly two million dollars. *The Atlantic Advocate*, possibly the only magazine established in Canada since the war, is a real success, serving the Eastern provinces, with large and growing circulation in the West.

Wardell has developed style in public speaking and he is addicted to the practice. He has the divine quality of listening quite as much as he talks. He has high spirits and emphatic and vigorous opinions, tenaciously held. It was natural that James Dunn should be drawn to this attractive companion.

Dunn's own conversation was marked by good humour and, although his witticisms are not easily quoted, he was never dull, with an unusual turn of phrase.

He had a tremendous power of narrative, marked by humour in abounding measure.

His writing on the other hand was pedantic. If he had been capable of writing as brilliantly as he talked, he would have been a remarkable novelist.

He often flew from Pennfield to Quebec—a distance of 250 miles—at 6.30 in the morning, just for a breakfast at the Château Frontenac with Maurice Duplessis, the Premier of that Province. They discussed Algoma and national

and international affairs—and they also argued
at length over the relative benefits of New
Brunswick and Quebec honey.

On his last visit in September, 1955, James
took with him a pot of special honey and, as
usual, Duplessis insisted that he should try a
pot of the local product which he considered far
superior to the honey from New Brunswick.

After breakfast, they would walk together on
the ramparts and talk of the past, not the immediate past, but that which was long distant.

Duplessis was proud of claiming some connection with Cardinal Richelieu, and indeed the
Prelate's portrait hung in his room.

He also had a fine timepiece of ancient fame
that was inscribed "Christopher 1451-1506".
The Christopher concerned was Columbus, but
James would never tire of trying to secure this
wonderful chronometer for Lady Dunn.

These early morning journeys to Quebec were
characteristic of him. Dunn always yearned to
be in the open air when the sun came up, and
on most days he was. Travelling made little
difference to his habits in this respect. He would
welcome the rising sun with equal enthusiasm
from the top deck of an ocean liner, from the
wide open window of some penthouse perched
above a great city—or on a beach when the little
fishing boats came in from their night's catch.

The sunrise seemed to refresh him and enable
him to meet the decisions and demands of the
new day, which never contained less than four-

teen hours devoted to work. How could he maintain such a long-sustained application to tasks?

His secret was that he knew what he was working for and, like Cromwell's Ironsides, he loved what he knew.

Although he passed for a singularly healthy and strong example of manhood, boasting he would live to great old age, he was in fact an ailing patient in those latter years. As I have related in this narrative, he was compelled to undergo serious surgical operations and he suffered a coronary thrombosis. I have told that he always concealed from his associates the nature and extent of his physical trials.

He suppressed the news of his indispositions from press and public in the belief that otherwise his authority over his Company's affairs would suffer damage.

Long after the need for secrecy had been dissipated by time and financial strength, his strange hallucination persisted and reached a climax on September 11, 1952, when he was within six weeks of his 78th birthday.

On that day he underwent a hernia operation. So that no one should know how serious it had been, he insisted on walking out of hospital on the following day. Dr. Greig, who attended James, then and always, did not get off as lightly as his patient. On his way home, after completing the operation, his motor car overturned and five of his twenty-five ribs were broken.

Dunn was no passive patient who accepted what he was told by the doctors; he actually enjoyed the intricacies of his restoration to health.

He was, in fact, intensely interested in all medical matters. Those years with good Doctor Duncan in his youth had left an abiding deposit of curiosity. Like so many men, Dunn was at heart a frustrated doctor. He always listened with attention to medical advice, especially when it dealt with diet, and he never followed doctors blindly when important issues of health were at stake.

He laid down the theory that the relationship between himself and his doctor was of an equal partnership. And he was no sleeping partner.

Meanwhile the distrust that had bedevilled the relations between C. D. Howe and James Dunn in the first three years of the War had long since given way to close personal contacts, and their social relations were warm and generous.

In 1947 James decided to rebuild a blast furnace. He asked Howe for a special ruling providing for a three-year write-off against income and excess profits taxes of the total cost, estimated at $340,000. This proposal went so much beyond the standard rates allowed for new plant that Howe took the precaution of seeking Cabinet approval. He wrote to James on April 4 a "private and confidential" letter telling him "a satisfactory decision of the Cabinet has been obtained." A copy of the Cabinet conclusion was attached.

In 1953 Dunn made for the first time an offer to Howe of the Algoma Chairmanship.*

In the same year Howe was taking a lively interest in Algoma affairs. On June 22, on the eve of the Canadian general election, he wrote a letter to Dunn, who was in London, giving an account of a conversation with Mr. Rodgie Mc-Lagan, President of the Algoma-controlled Canada Steamships. Howe reported labour troubles and delays in movement of iron ore. A collision resulting in the sinking of another freighter gave some concern.

In the last days of August in the last full year of his life, James visited Clarence Dillon at Dark Harbour in Maine. It was, too, the last time he looked upon his old friend.

In mid-September he went to Toronto, where he signed the third codicil to his will, restoring his son Philip to his list of executors and adding C. D. Howe and Lady Dunn's sister Olymbia.

On October 14, 1955, Howe, who had served in Government as a Cabinet Minister for twenty years, told Dunn that he would like to retire. James at once renewed the offer of the Chairmanship of Algoma. Howe replied that he would like to take a "rain check". It was Dunn's last offer to Howe.

The 29th of October 1955 was James's last birthday.

---

* The sequel to this friendly association between Dunn and Howe is told in the Appendix—Estate of Sir James Dunn.

Mr. and Mrs. Howe arrived in the afternoon and stayed on with the Dunns for several days. The airplane *Victoria* was sent to Fredericton to bring me to Dayspring in St. Andrews. James received hundreds of telegrams and letters of congratulations.

Dr. Greig was one of the guests. He examined James thoroughly and reported that everything was most satisfactory.

In his eighty-second year, there was no notice, no premonition of the darkness that would shortly possess him.

That evening we sat down to a great birthday dinner with many different dishes and bottles of rare wines. A film display in the private cinema concluded the celebrations.

We met again in New York on December 2. James and Christofor both dined with me in my rooms at the Waldorf Towers and next evening I dined with them at the Pavillon Restaurant.

It was our last meeting. There was no warning that the association begun so many years ago on the North Shore of the Province by the sea was drawing to a close. There was no unfolding of vision that the boys who had lived through childhood, middle age and old age would be parted, and that I would be left to finish the journey alone.

On the following day, James and Christofor flew to Washington and there they joined George Humphrey, the Secretary of the Treasury, at his home.

James was in good humour with abundant vitality. He was so absorbed in conversation with George Humphrey that he hardly noticed the food he was eating!

Humphrey took them both to dine with Sinclair Weeks, Secretary of Commerce, and James enjoyed a good many tots of bourbon. Everyone declared that he had never looked better. But his appearance of health was deceptive. That night he was restless, his pulse rapid.

James claimed he had climbed the steep stairs to his room slowly, though very short of breath. He was most anxious to return to Dayspring at once.

There was a ground fog with a thin drizzle, and it appeared doubtful whether they could make the journey in these bad flying conditions. But Christofor insisted that they should take off, and try to reach Montreal. As the plane took wing, snow began to fall.

A tail wind helped them on their journey, and visibility cleared miraculously. They landed at Pennfield near their home.

For five days James kept to his bed. But he was as restless as ever and would carry on long and involved telephone conversations with executives at Algoma. And all the while he was breathless, as though he had been running uphill.

On December 11 Dunn complained of pain.

On the following day Christofor sent their airplane *Victoria* to collect Dr. Oille at Toronto and Dr. Greig from the Sault. The doctors spent three days with their patient. They played Chinese chequers and he talked about Algoma.

Sometimes they would vary the game by playing backgammon. James usually won. He had been a backgammon player since his days at Dalhousie.

The doctors reported that James was suffering from extreme fatigue, and said that if only he could relax it would be the best medicine of all. They were convinced he would recover swiftly and after a few days they returned to the West.

We had agreed that James and Christofor would join me for Christmas at my house in the West Indies. But the weather was too bad for travelling. They stayed at Dayspring.

On Christmas night James walked about the house from room to room as though treasuring in his mind a last memory of the home that had been so dear to him and which he loved more than any other place in the world. Then at night on the 28th of December he came into Christofor's room. The light of a cold white moon was streaming through the window. He stood looking at her for a long time, bathed in this light, as though imprinting on his mind the memory of her face. When he spoke it was in a whisper, almost as though he was thinking aloud.

"I have shot my bolt," he said quietly. "I think I have shot my bolt."

She began talking excitedly of many things in an effort to change his train of thought.

The telephone rang: it was Rodgie McLagan

of Canada Steamships. As they talked of old, familiar things, James sounded himself again.

Christofor, however, called Dr. Oille and urged him to return to Dayspring at once, bringing Dr. Greig.

Dr. Greig was delayed by the storm, but James's friend Oille arrived on the following evening and examined his patient with minute care. He reported that nothing had deteriorated. At dinner, James had a good appetite.

Afterwards, he asked for a small brandy, but did not drink it. He put it down untouched and went to his bedroom. Christofor followed him, and at once called for Dr. Oille.

James Dunn was lying across the bed in exactly the same position as in 1941. Holding his chest, he complained of indigestion.

Dr. Oille was standing in the doorway, watching them.

He tried to calm his patient by persuading James that his pains must be only indigestion, and too high up to have anything to do with his heart.

Suddenly, as they talked, there was a gurgling noise in James's throat. As each breath came and went it was as though waters were in turmoil.

The doctor rushed out of the room and returned with a hypodermic of morphine. As the drug took effect, the laboured breathing grew quieter.

James regained command of himself on the

Friday morning, and turned to Dr. Oille to ask one question.

"How long have I got?" he asked. "I want to say goodbye to Christofor."

Dr. Oille said nothing. James looked across to the woman who had meant so much to him.

"Hallo, kid," he said gently. "Don't let me go." These were his last words.

No one could now delay or stay the passing of his great spirit. All that medicine and love could do had already been done. And on the first day of the New Year life left the strong body of which he had rightly been so proud, and his soul voyaged on into the eternal mists.

In Algoma, seven hundred miles to the west, the steel mills rolled on, the iron mines gave forth their wealth, and countless thousands of workers and dependents drew their livelihood from the enterprise which James Dunn had built up from ruin.

In Montreal, the financial centre of the East, when the news spread that the man had died who created the wealth which was the basis of their speculations, the price of Algoma Common leapt from 93 to 103.

So ended a long and marvellous life.

James Hamet Dunn, the boy from Bathurst, the man who saw a vision and worked to make it come true—how will he be remembered?

His character was so rich, so many-sided that every one of his friends praises him for a different reason—and considers that theirs is the best.

As with all great personalities, he was not only one man, but many. He was too big, too colourful, too exuberant to fit easily into any simple classification.

He knew how to use old age and filled it with "gracious living", for himself and for those about him. The years did not quench the noble fires within him.

The chief memorial to James Dunn is the vast Algoma enterprise. He breathed life into a dying organization; he guided Algoma out of the shadows into the realms of gold and glory. He demonstrated that Old Age was no barrier to achievement. At 61 he entered upon his Kingdom and for twenty years he ruled. By the development of ore bodies he fired all Canada with enthusiasm for exploration and research. His example was responsible for the launching of many projects that have increased and even multiplied the mineral wealth of Canada. In thousands of homes in Sault Ste Marie, he is remembered as the man who brought them prosperity and drove out fear and hunger. To hundreds of thousands more, he is the man whose faith, resourcefulness, and genius also brought into being a great steel company.

But no memorial can recall the individual qualities by which his friends remember him. No words can do justice to his kindness and humanity. He was possessed of the rare simplicity that only goes with real greatness of character.

He was always frank and outspoken. He lived openly and he felt deeply. Nothing was held back. He had the good graces of mockery and impish fun. He was free from solemnity. He could call names with the worst, and yet no one was as insistent in observing the courtesies of life. He talked brilliantly. And sometimes he said too much. But he did not surround himself with those who were only good listeners. His talk was best when he had a single companion. In a large gathering he was apt to listen too much, and too long.

He sought out and held the attention of many distinguished men; men of the calibre of Asquith, F. E. Smith, Bonar Law, Churchill, Bracken and others. He was not a sinner, but he liked the company of sinners. His standards of conduct did not exclude a partiality for jovial friendships and high-spirited companionship. He had, too, an exuberance of character which reminded me of F. E. Smith and Churchill.

He was pugnacious and yet he never harboured rancour. Unswerving in his devotion to his friends. Dwelling always on the mountain peak or in the valley, he gave out gloom or glory, pessimism or complete triumph.

He began as a young man in a hurry: too impatient and too ambitious. His character broadened with the years, and was strengthened as he won fame, and prosperity. He displayed an insight and astuteness which marked him out as a foremost industrial leader. He had the far-reaching imagination of one who could see beyond present difficulties to future greatness. And he developed the tenacity that gives substance to faith.

James Dunn enriched us in the example he set of perseverance and generosity. His was the lonely and serene steadfastness of the leader. His compassion flowed like Niagara. His other emotions of love and hate and anger were on the same scale.

He was my very dear friend for nearly three-quarters of a century, and a joyous companion on the way. He was a son of the Province by the Sea, who lived and worked for all Canada.

His life began in Canada, was continued in England and came to an end in Canada.

In Canada were the modest beginnings. In Canada, too, the mighty triumph.

James Dunn's was a life lived fully, creatively and daringly on both shores of the ocean. And on both shores will his name be remembered in honour among men.

APPENDIX I

SIR JAMES DUNN'S ESTATE

AT THE TIME of Sir James Dunn's death in 1956, his net assets were valued at $65,825,000. His holding in Algoma steel alone was worth $64,855,000. Thus it accounted for almost all the estate.

There were shareholdings in other concerns amounting to $3,136,000.

There was one significant liability: loans from banks amounted to $2,253,000. This may seem a strange debt for a man worth more than sixty million dollars. But it shows that Sir James Dunn was taking the good advice he gave Mr. George Humphrey in 1950, when he counselled his American friend to borrow money from the bank against any shares deposited with it.*

The Will was dated 19th of January 1950 and was signed in New York.

The executors and trustees were Lady Dunn, Philip Dunn, Gordon McMillan, Dr. Herbert Greig, David Holbrook and Frank Harris. James authorized them to postpone the conversion of the estate.

A codicil of 16th of February 1954 named Rodgie McLagan an additional executor and trustee. Dunn also gave authority to his executors to postpone the sale of his Algoma shares until 1975.

A second codicil of February 1955 revoked the first codicil, removed the executors and trustees and named instead Lady Dunn, Gordon McMillan and David Holbrook, giving to Lady Dunn and Mr. McMillan power to postpone the sale of his Algoma shares until 1975.

The third and last codicil of the 13th of September 1955 revoked the list of executors and trustees and named instead Lady Dunn, C. D. Howe, Philip Dunn, Olympia Kedros and Gordon McMillan.

The appointment of Mr. Howe showed how an old hostility had turned into friendship and intimacy. For

---

* See page 193.

Howe, the appointment involved some degree of embarrassment. He was a Federal Cabinet Minister, head of a department which from time to time bought steel from Algoma. Besides, the payment of substantial fees to executors was an obligation laid by law upon the estate. Plainly the situation was one of some delicacy for Howe.

But having surrendered any claim on these fees, a considerable sacrifice, he was advised that it would be proper for him to act as executor.

After the defeat of the Liberal Government and of Mr. Howe in his own constituency, he visited Lady Dunn at Dayspring. He said he had suffered a terrible blow and was nothing more than a discarded politician. Within the year Lady Dunn was committed to a Science Building for Dalhousie University at a cost of over two million dollars and Mr. Howe at a special meeting of Governors was appointed the first Chancellor of this prominent and important institute of learning.

His administration was distinguished by expansion of the Faculties and particularly the Law Faculty, which has been endowed by Lady Dunn. She has provided seven Law scholarships yearly of $1,500 each and also a librarian, secretary and cataloguer, representing an annual expenditure of about fifteen thousand dollars, a total annual sum of twenty-five thousand five hundred dollars.

As for the division of the estate: one half was bequeathed to Sir James Dunn's widow—who was in her own right already a wealthy woman—and one-twelfth to each of his five children and one grandchild, Mona's daughter.

Lady Dunn and Mr. McMillan did not avail themselves of authority to defer the sale of Algoma shares for over twenty-five years. Death duties which amounted to $35,775,000 forced the distribution of large blocks of stock.

APPENDIX II

SECURITIES HELD BY SIR JAMES DUNN AT HIS DEATH

	No. of shares	Value in dollars
Algoma Steel Corporation	702,086	$64,855,000
Algoma Central and Hudson's Bay Railway Co. (Common)	14,560	437,000
Aluminium Ltd. (Common)	7,703	832,000
Bathurst Power and Paper Co. (Class B)	6,000	228,000
Canada Steamship Lines (Common)	5,500	184,000
(Preferred)	13,270	172,000
Cassiar Asbestos Corporation (Common)	2,000	18,000
Consolidated Paper Corporation (Common)	9,050	324,000
East Sullivan Mines	5,000	25,000
Fraser Companies Ltd. (Common)	4,375	140,000
General Dynamics Corporation	500	33,000
International Nickel Co. of Canada (Common)	1,500	123,000
Page-Hersey Tube Ltd. (Common)	450	36,000
White Motor Co. (Common)	575	22,000
Brown Company (Common)	8,000	144,000
Price Bros. & Co. Ltd. (Common)	5,850	316,000
Algoma Central and H. B. Railway (Preferred)	1,597	2,000
(5% Bonds)	61,600 (dollars)	100,000
		$67,991,000

APPENDIX III

CHRONOLOGICAL TABLE

1874	Born
1894	Loisette and first visit to England
1895	Enrolls at Dalhousie
1898	Graduation
1900	Joins firm of Greenshields
1901	Marries Gertrude Price
1902	Becomes a member of the Montreal Stock Exchange
1903	Meets F. S. Pearson
1905	Sets up London Office
1907	Meets Clergue and becomes involved in Algoma
1908	Fleming buys up bankrupt Algoma
1909	Association with Loewenstein begins
1913	Fischer defaults
1914	Hospital trip to battle lines
1915	Death of Pearson
1915-17	Norway and nickel consignments
1921	Baronet
1926	Marries Irene, Lady Queensberry
1928	Death of Loewenstein
1928	Death of Dunn's daughter Mona
1933	Boots' shares purchased
1934-35	Algoma reorganization
1935	Becomes President and Chairman of Algoma
1935	Miss Christoforides appointed Assistant Secretary
1937	Bank crisis. Royal Bank takes over account
1938	Algoma shares listed on Montreal and Toronto Stock Exchanges
1939	War and tremendous efforts by Algoma
1941	Thrombosis

1941	Fear of attacks on management of Algoma and menaced by attempts to seize control
1942	Marries Marcia Christoforides
1943	Second illness at Toronto—Prostate operation Government attack on Algoma Management
1944	Escape from Hanna contract
1944	Voting control of Algoma assured
1945	Purchased Dayspring
1947	Government Controls abandoned
1950	Sale of Algoma shares to Coal and Ore Companies
1950	Sale of Algoma shares to Hanna
1952	Illness at Sault—hernia operation
1955	Last will—Howe named Executor
1956	Death

INDEX